The Communal First Saturdays Devotional

In reparation for the sins committed against the Immaculate Heart of Mary for the salvation of souls and peace in the world

A guide for participating each month in the *First Saturdays* communally (can also be adapted for individual use)

by First Saturdays for Peace

"Have compassion on the Heart of your Most Holy Mother covered with the thorns with which ungrateful men pierce it at every moment, and there is no one to remove them with an act of reparation."
(The Child Jesus to Sr. Lucia, December 10, 1925)

First Edition May 13, 2017
Second Edition August 15, 2017
Third Edition January 25, 2021

Email:
info@communalfirstsaturdays.org

www.CommunalFirstSaturdays.org

ISBN: 978-1-951233-02-0

In reparation for the sins committed against the Immaculate Heart of Mary

The Communal First Saturdays Devotional

Contents

Appendix I
The Pilgrim Virgin Statue Church to Home Visitation

Contents

Appendix II
The Reception of the Brown Scapular

Appendix III
Hymns

1. Outline of a Model Communal First Saturday

-1:00   **Individual Confessions**
-0:40   Communal devotion begins with intentions and prayers
-0:30   **The Rosary**
0:00   **The Holy Sacrifice of the Mass** with **Communion of reparation**
0:30   **Scripture Meditation** on the mysteries of the Rosary while keeping Our Lady company
0:50   Litany and Prayers for the Holy Father
0:55   Reception of the Pilgrim Virgin Statue in the Church *(optional)*
1:00   Reception of the Brown Scapular *(optional)*

0:00 represents whatever the actual starting time for Holy Mass is in the particular parish or community. Thus, the Rosary is 30 minutes before the starting time for the Holy Mass, the intentions and prayers begin 40 minutes earlier than the start of the Holy Mass, and the lectio divina meditation with Scripture would begin after the conclusion of the Holy Mass (about 30 minutes after the starting time for the Holy Mass). The Litany of the Blessed Virgin Mary and prayers for the Holy Father follow.

Other recommended devotions, such as the Pilgrim Virgin Statue Church to Home Visitation, would begin after the litany and prayers for the Holy Father (about 55 minutes after the starting time for the Holy Mass). If there is the Reception of the Brown Scapular, it would take place last, either after the reception of the Pilgrim Virgin Statue or after the Prayers for the Holy Father. If possible, individual Confessions would begin an hour or more before the Holy Mass. One would need to check the parish schedule for actual times. All times are approximate.

2. The Order for the Communal First Saturdays

For further explanation of the Order of Devotion see Appendix G of "The Communal First Saturdays" book.

2.1 Individual Confession *(Sacrament of Penance and Reconciliation), the first of four practices with the intention of making reparation to the Immaculate Heart of Mary*

2.11 Prayers before Confession *(optional)*

To Mary, Refuge of Sinners

O Immaculate Heart of Mary, in the fire of love which burns in Thee, may all my sins be consumed and all my affections purified. Let me by true penitence draw out the painful thorns with which I have pierced thee. May something of that divine fire of love which fills thee, enter my heart so that my service of thy Son may be complete. In lasting devotion to thy Immaculate Heart may I be willing to share its sorrows now, so that seeing thee in Heaven I may possess some of the blessed joy which thy Son imparts to it. Immaculate Heart of Mary, I am thine in sorrow and joy, in time and eternity. Amen.

(Fr. Thomas McGlynn, OP, July 24, 1958)

To Jesus, Fountain of Mercy

Heart of Jesus through the Immaculate Heart of Mary in union with St. Joseph and with the help of all the Angels and Saints, pour forth Your Holy Spirit into my heart so as to shed Your light upon all my sins. Grant me true repentance for all of my sins which have offended You, and that I may detest all my sins, even venial ones. Grant me the grace to strive to make reparation for all of my sins and the sins of others, which offend the Most Holy Trinity. Through this Sacrament may I also try to repair the sins that specifically offend Your Sacred Heart and the Immaculate Heart of Mary.

Psalm 51

Prayer for Cleansing and Pardon

51 Have mercy on me, O God, according to thy steadfast love;
according to thy abundant mercy blot out my transgressions.
[2] Wash me thoroughly from my iniquity,
and cleanse me from my sin!

[3] For I know my transgressions,
and my sin is ever before me.
[4] Against thee, thee only, have I sinned,
and done that which is evil in thy sight,
so that thou art justified in thy sentence
and blameless in thy judgment.
[5] Behold, I was brought forth in iniquity,
and in sin did my mother conceive me.

[6] Behold, thou desirest truth in the inward being;
therefore teach me wisdom in my secret heart.

[7] Purge me with hyssop, and I shall be clean;
   wash me, and I shall be whiter than snow.
[8] Fill me with joy and gladness;
let the bones which thou hast broken rejoice.
[9] Hide thy face from my sins,
   and blot out all my iniquities.

[10] Create in me a clean heart, O God,
   and put a new and right spirit within me.
[11] Cast me not away from thy presence,
   and take not thy holy Spirit from me.
[12] Restore to me the joy of thy salvation,
   and uphold me with a willing spirit.

[13] Then I will teach transgressors thy ways,
   and sinners will return to thee.
[14] Deliver me from bloodguiltiness, O God,
   thou God of my salvation,
and my tongue will sing aloud of thy deliverance.

[15] O Lord, open thou my lips,
   and my mouth shall show forth thy praise.
[16] For thou hast no delight in sacrifice;
were I to give a burnt offering, thou wouldst not be pleased.
[17] The sacrifice acceptable to God is a broken spirit;
a broken and contrite heart, O God, thou wilt not despise.

[18] Do good to Zion in thy good pleasure;
   rebuild the walls of Jerusalem,
[19] then wilt thou delight in right sacrifices,
   in burnt offerings and whole burnt offerings;
   then bulls will be offered on thy altar.

2.12 Examination of Conscience

It is not the intention of this book to provide a particular method of examination of conscience since this can vary with the needs of different people and can vary as well with the same person as one journeys through the various stages of the spiritual life. One might apply some of the aids below as a help for examining one's conscience (cf. also the Catechism of the Catholic Church). As a final step, before Confession, we recommend the "Prayer of Intention for Confession" on page 7.

The Ten Commandments may be studied further in order to provide a more thorough framework for self-examination. The Beatitudes also provide a helpful examination for making spiritual progress. In order to trace numerous specific sins back to their roots in the heart, it is helpful to reflect on the seven capital sins.

It is also helpful to reflect on and develop the virtues listed as well as others, about which we can learn more, as for example, through spiritual reading. These virtues and many others reach an extraordinary degree of perfection in the Immaculate Heart of Mary. In a way, we can look into the Heart of Mary to see if we have failed in these virtues, either by acts contrary to them or by omission. In the Immaculate Heart of Mary we find the way that we should respond to the Sacred Heart of Jesus and be joined to Him. The gifts and fruits of the Holy Spirit are also to be found in the Immaculate Heart of Mary in great perfection without the least blemish. Finally, the precepts of the Church provide us with a reminder of our minimum duty as Catholics.

For further information, refer to the question and answer concerning the necessity of forming one's conscience (cf. "The Communal First Saturdays" book, Part II, Section One, Ch. 2, q. 19). One should not put off going to Confession because one might not be confident about doing everything perfectly. One simply takes the first step, and then another will follow. The priest is present in the confessional to help the penitent make a good confession.

The Ten Commandments

1. I am the LORD your GOD: You shall not have strange gods before me.
2. You shall not take the name of the LORD your GOD in vain.
3. Remember to keep holy the LORD'S day.
4. Honor your father and your mother.
5. You shall not kill.
6. You shall not commit adultery.
7. You shall not steal.
8. You shall not bear false witness against your neighbor.
9. You shall not covet your neighbor's wife.
10. You shall not covet your neighbor's goods.
(cf. *Catechism of the Catholic Church*, 2nd edition, pp. 496-7, cf. Ex. 20:2-17, cf. Dt. 5, 6-21).

The Beatitudes

Blessed are the poor in spirit, for theirs is the kingdom of Heaven.
Blessed are those who mourn, for they shall be comforted.
Blessed are the meek, for they shall inherit the earth.
Blessed are those who hunger and thirst for righteousness, for they shall be satisfied.
Blessed are the merciful, for they shall obtain mercy.
Blessed are the pure in heart, for they shall see God.
Blessed are the peacemakers, for they shall be called sons of God.
Blessed are those who are persecuted for righteousness' sake, for theirs is the kingdom of heaven.
Blessed are you when men revile you and persecute you and utter all kinds of evil against you falsely on my account. Rejoice and be glad, for your reward is great in heaven, for so men persecuted the prophets who were before you (Mt. 5:3-12).

The Seven Capital Sins

The seven capital or root sins: pride, avarice (greed), envy, wrath, lust, gluttony, and sloth. "They are called 'capital' because they engender other sins, other vices" (*Catechism of the Catholic Church*, n. 1866). "God opposes the proud, but gives grace to the humble" (Jas. 4:6).

The Virtues

The virtues: Faith, Hope, Love, Religion, Justice, Prudence, Fortitude, Temperance, Chastity, Humility, Patience, Kindness, and a multitude of others (cf. *Catechism of the Catholic Church*, n. 1803-1828). Love or Charity "binds everything together in perfect harmony" (Col. 3:14, cf. I Cor. 13:13, cf. also Gal. 5:18-25).

Gifts and Fruits of the Holy Spirit

The Catechism of the Catholic Church helps us to acknowledge the essential gifts and fruits of the Holy Spirit for our sanctification so that we can examine the behavior that does not correspond to them:

5

The moral life of Christians is sustained by the gifts of the Holy Spirit. These are permanent dispositions which make man docile in following the promptings of the Holy Spirit (n. 1830).

The seven *gifts* of the Holy Spirit are wisdom, understanding, counsel, fortitude, knowledge, piety, and fear of the Lord. They belong in their fullness to Christ, Son of David. They complete and perfect the virtues of those who receive them. They make the faithful docile in readily obeying divine inspirations (n. 1831).

"Let your good spirit lead me on a level path" (Ps. 143:10, n. 1831).

"For all who are led by the Spirit of God are sons of God . . . If children, then heirs, heirs of God and fellow heirs with Christ" (Rom 8:14, 17, n. 1831).

The *fruits* of the Spirit are perfections that the Holy Spirit forms in us as the first fruits of eternal glory. The tradition of the Church lists twelve of them: 'charity, joy, peace, patience, kindness, goodness, generosity, gentleness, faithfulness, modesty, self-control, chastity' (Gal. 5:22-23, n. 1832).

The Greatest Commandment in the Law

And he said to him, "**You shall love the Lord your God with all your heart, and with all your soul, and with all your mind.** This is the great and first commandment. And a second is like it, **You shall love your neighbor as yourself.** On these two commandments depend all the law and the prophets" (Mt. 22:37-40, emphasis ours).

The Precepts of the Church

The precepts of the Church are Church laws which we are obligated to obey. In this way, the Church as a loving Mother guides us along a path that serves not only our good but the good of others. The Church's power to make laws is included in the words: "...Whatever you bind on earth, shall be bound in heaven..." (Mt. 16:19, 18:18). "The Catechism of the Catholic Church" tells us:

The first precept ("You shall attend Mass on Sundays and on holy days of obligation and rest from servile labor") requires the faithful to participate in the Eucharistic celebration when the Christian community gathers together on the day commemorating the Resurrection of the Lord...

The second precept ("You shall confess your sins at least once a year.") ensures preparation for the Eucharist by the reception of the sacrament of reconciliation, which continues Baptism's work of conversion and forgiveness.

The third precept ("You shall receive the sacrament of the Eucharist at least during the Easter season.") guarantees as a minimum the reception of the Lord's Body and Blood in connection with the Paschal feasts, the origin and center of the Christian liturgy.

The fourth precept ("You shall observe the days of fasting and abstinence established by the Church") ensures the times of ascesis and penance which prepare us for the liturgical feasts and help us acquire mastery over our instincts and freedom of heart.

The fifth precept ("You shall help to provide for the needs of the Church") means that the faithful are obliged to assist with the material needs of the Church, each according to his own ability (*Catechism of the Catholic Church*, 2042-2043).

The precepts of the Church are an "indispensable minimum" for leading a Catholic life.

Prayer of Intention for Confession

O Jesus, this is for love of You, for the conversion of sinners, for the Holy Father, and in reparation for the sins committed against the Immaculate Heart of Mary. (Cf. 2.23).

2.13 During Confession

Make the Sign of the Cross.

Be open to the priest's direction.

You may tell the priest your state of life (single, married, religious, etc.). Tell how long it has been since your last Confession (weeks, months, years, etc.).

(It is not required to mention the additional intention of making reparation to the Immaculate Heart of Mary in the confessional).

Confess all mortal sins that you have not confessed and the number of times that you committed them. You are encouraged to confess your venial sins. Listen to what the priest says (which includes the penance given, to at least make partial reparation for your sins).

2.14 Act of Contrition

Pray an act of contrition as directed. There are many forms of an act of contrition that one may choose to pray. Here are three forms of an expression of sorrow for one's sins, which one may use. The first form may be helpful to those attempting to gain a plenary indulgence, since one of the conditions is detachment from all sin. This can be expressed through the words "I detest all my sins."

My God, I am deeply sorry in my heart for having offended You, and I detest all my sins because I dread the loss of Heaven and the pains of Hell. But most of all because they offend You my God Who are all good and deserving of all my love. I firmly resolve with the help of Your grace to sin no more, to do penance, and to avoid the occasions of sin. Amen (*Reconciliation: A Short Guide,* www.USCCB.org).

Or:

My God, I am sorry for my sins with all my heart. In choosing to do wrong and failing to do good, I have sinned against you whom I should love above all things. I firmly intend, with your help, to do penance, to sin no more, and to avoid whatever leads me to sin. Our Savior Jesus Christ suffered and died for us. In his name, my God, have mercy (*Rite of Penance*).

Or:

Father, I have sinned against you and am not worthy to be called your son. Be merciful to me a sinner (*Rite of Penance*, Lk. 15:18, 18:13).

Acting in the person of Christ, the priest can give the absolution from sin.

2.15 After Confession

Perform the penance given by the priest in satisfaction (reparation) for your sins. This will, at least, satisfy partially for the temporal punishment due to your sins. Certainly all of one's sins are forgiven by the absolution. Yet temporal punishment may still remain and may only be partially satisfied by the penance (cf. Catechism of the Catholic Church, n. 1459-1460).

Recall the advice of the Priest and try to act on it.

For additional practical information on the Sacrament of Penance go to the U.S. Conference of Catholic Bishops website at www.usccb.org. Search under "Sacrament of Penance." In other countries, one might search for the particular national conference of Bishops website.

2.2 Communal Order of Devotion and Liturgy

The leader should not read out loud any instructions which are in italics (cf. Appendix F of "The Communal First Saturdays" book). For additional information, please see Appendix G of the same book.

If applicable, the Pilgrim Virgin statue could process in and be placed in the sanctuary or other authorized location, before the devotion begins. If a procession is not possible, the statue could be simply placed in the authorized location.

2.21 Introduction: The Child Jesus and His Mother Speak to Us

Leader: *Greeting*

Leader: We will now begin the Communal Order of Devotion and Liturgy. Please turn your books to page 10.

Begin by making the Sign of the Cross.

9

Leader: In the Name of the Father and of the Son and of the Holy Spirit. Amen.

The Child Jesus said to Sr. Lucia:

"Have compassion on the Heart of your Most Holy Mother covered with the thorns with which ungrateful men pierce it at every moment, and there is no one to remove them with an act of reparation."
Our Lady then said:
"My daughter, look at My Heart surrounded with the thorns with which ungrateful men pierce it at every moment by their blasphemies and ingratitude. You at least try to console me, and say that I promise to assist at the hour of death with all the graces necessary for salvation all those who on the first Saturday of five consecutive months, go to Confession and receive Holy Communion, recite five decades of the Rosary and keep me company for a quarter of an hour while meditating on the mysteries of the Rosary, with the intention of making reparation to me" *(December 10, 1925)*.

Sr. Lucia later asked Jesus if it would be all right to go to Confession within eight days. Jesus replied, "Yes, and it could be longer still, provided that, when they receive me, they are in the state of grace and have the intention of making reparation to the Immaculate Heart of Mary" *(February 15, 1926).*

2.22 Intentions for the Communal First Saturdays

The following intentions for the Communal First Saturdays are not meant to be understood as General Intercessions but rather as an aid to fulfilling Our Lady's request. For example, one could easily try to fulfill the four practices of the First Saturdays and forget to make the intention of making reparation to the Immaculate Heart of Mary, which is an essential part of the devotion. Thus, the following intentions help us to fulfill the conditions of the First Saturdays with the proper intention. There are also five additional intentions that are helpful in fulfilling Our Lady's request.

Leader: Please join me in making the following intentions for the *Communal First Saturdays.*

All: To offer reparation to the Most Holy Trinity for all sins.

All: To go to Confession with the intention of making reparation to the Immaculate Heart of Mary;

All: To receive Jesus with love in Holy Communion with the intention of making reparation to the Immaculate Heart of Mary;

All: To pray the Rosary with the intention of making reparation to the Immaculate Heart of Mary;

All: To keep Our Lady company while meditating for fifteen minutes on the mysteries of the Rosary with the intention of making reparation to the Immaculate Heart of Mary;

All: For the grace to practice and fulfill Our Lord and Our Lady's request for the five First Saturdays and to continue to practice them for the salvation of others and peace in the world;

All: To try to make reparation to the Immaculate Heart of Mary for the sins against her Immaculate Conception, Virginity, Divine Motherhood and Spiritual Maternity, children's love for her, and Sacred Images.

All: That the reparation we make to the Sacred Heart of Jesus and the Immaculate Heart of Mary may console Them.

All: That all of our sufferings and the many sufferings throughout the world, past, present, and future, may help to serve as reparation to the Hearts of Jesus and His Mother.

All: To offer reparation for all the sins against Holy Mother Church and against our brothers and sisters throughout the world.

All: That we may gain any indulgences offered by Holy Mother Church.

2.23 Prayers before the Rosary

Fatima Prayers

Leader: Let us say the Fatima prayers together.

All: My God, I believe, I adore, I hope, and I love You; I ask pardon of You for those who do not believe, do not adore, do not hope, and do not love You.

All: Most Holy Trinity, Father, Son, and Holy Spirit I adore You profoundly. I offer You the Most Precious Body, Blood, Soul, and Divinity of Jesus Christ, present in all the tabernacles throughout the world, in reparation for the outrages, sacrileges, and indifference by which He is offended. And through the infinite merits of His most Sacred Heart, and of the Immaculate Heart of Mary, I beg the conversion of poor sinners.

All: O Most Holy Trinity, I adore You. My God, my God, I love You in the most Blessed Sacrament.

All: O Jesus, this is for love of You, for the conversion of sinners, for the Holy Father, and in reparation for the sins committed against the Immaculate Heart of Mary. *(Jacinta added "the Holy Father.")*

All: O my Jesus, forgive us our sins, save us from the fires of hell; lead all souls to Heaven, especially those in most need of Thy mercy.

All: Sweet Heart of Mary be my salvation!

The leader can announce each of the following prayers.

Leader: Act of Consecration to the Sacred Heart of Jesus through the Immaculate Heart of Mary

All: Heavenly Father, You so loved us that you sent Your only begotten Son Who emptied Himself, taking the form of a slave in the womb of the Blessed Virgin Mary by the power of the Holy Spirit for our salvation. Grant that as Jesus made a total Gift of Himself in His Sacrifice on the Cross, we may make a total return of ourselves to You through the Sacred Heart of Your Son and with the intercession of the Immaculate Heart of Mary.

Loving Jesus, grant that we may renew our personal consecration to You this day, a consecration that began with our Baptism. By that same Baptism, we acknowledge that we are totally yours and all we have is yours. Help us, loving Savior, to renew our baptismal promises to reject

Satan, to reject sin, and to profess the Catholic Faith no matter what the cost. May we serve you by our baptismal anointing as priest, prophet, and king through the intercession of the Maternal Heart of Your Mother. You have given her to us as our own that we may offer to You a perfect and Immaculate Heart.

Loving Mother, we entrust to your Immaculate Heart our entire being, body and soul, and all that we have internal and external. Through your Maternal mediation and by the grace of the Holy Spirit, join us to the Heart of your Son, so that through Him we may come to the Father.

Loving Jesus and Mary, grant that we may also fulfill your request for the First Saturdays. In this way, we hope, by the grace of the Holy Spirit, to obtain world peace and the salvation of souls, including our own. Amen.

Leader: **Act of Reparation to Jesus through the Immaculate Heart of Mary**

All: Most Holy Virgin Mother, we listen with grief to the pleas of your Child concerning your Immaculate Heart surrounded with the thorns placed therein at every moment by the blasphemies and ingratitude of humanity. We are moved by the ardent desire of loving you as Our Mother and of promoting a true devotion to your Immaculate Heart, especially by these Communions of reparation.

We therefore kneel before you to manifest the sorrow we experience for the grievances that we cause you, and to atone by our prayers and sacrifices for the offenses which have pierced your Heart and the Heart of your Son. Obtain for all of us the pardon of so many sins. Hasten the conversion of us sinners that we may love Jesus and cease to offend the Lord, Who is already so much offended. Turn your eyes of mercy toward us, that we may love God with all our hearts on earth and enjoy Him forever in Heaven. Amen.

Leader: **Prayer to St. Joseph**

All: Hail Joseph, shadow of the Father, guardian of the Redeemer, and protector of the way that leads to and through the Immaculate Heart of Mary, your true spouse. Please ask the Father to give us efficacious graces through the Heart of Jesus and by the Holy Spirit. Obtain by the intercession of the Heart of Mary that we faithfully fulfill Jesus and Mary's requests. Please present our offerings to and through the Immaculate Heart of Mary in reparation for the sins which have offended her and her Son. Inspire us to fulfill and spread the *First Saturdays* everywhere, so that many souls will be rescued from sin and be brought to eternal life.

Grant also as you blessed the world at Fatima with the Child Jesus, the Lamb of God, you bless us, and help us to build and maintain the civilization of love and peace which Our Lady has promised as the victory of her Immaculate Heart. For you are "…the faithful and wise servant, whom his master has set over his household, to give them their food at the proper time…" He set you "over all his possessions" *(Mt. 24:45, 47)*. Thus we too wish to be entrusted entirely to your care, as members of your household for the honor and glory of the Hearts of Jesus and Mary. Amen.

Leader: **Prayer for Protection of Conscience Rights and Religious Liberty (*USCCB*)**

Father, we praise you and thank you for your most precious gifts of human life and human freedom.
Touch the hearts of our lawmakers with the wisdom and courage to uphold conscience rights and religious liberty for all. Protect all people from being forced to violate their moral and religious convictions.
In your goodness, guard our freedom to live out our faith and to follow you in all that we do. Give us strength to be bold and joyful witnesses.
We ask this through Christ, our Lord. Amen.

Leader: Invocations of the Patrons of the Communal First Saturdays

All of these saints specifically named have a special connection with the Communal First Saturdays whether it be related to Fatima, the First Saturdays or some practice of the First Saturdays such as the Holy Eucharist, the Sacrament of Reconciliation, or the Rosary.

Leader:

St. Michael, the Archangel; *All: pray for us.*
St. Mary Magdalene; *pray for us.*
St. Dominic; *pray for us.*

St. Catherine of Siena; *pray for us.*
St. Thomas Aquinas; *pray for us.*
St. Anthony of Padua; *pray for us.*
St. John Mary Vianney; *All: pray for us.*
St. Padre Pio; *pray for us.*
St. John Paul II; *pray for us.*
Sts. Jacinta and Francisco; *pray for us.*
All you Angels and Saints of God; *pray for us.*

2.24 The Three Remaining Practices *for fulfilling the First Saturdays (Also see the first practice, individual Confession, above)*

1). The Rosary *with the intention of making reparation to the Immaculate Heart of Mary*

Recitation of the Rosary

Leader: Please speak at a moderate pace.

Leader: Please turn your books to page 15. We will now pray the Rosary with the intention of making reparation to the Immaculate Heart of Mary.

Begin by making the Sign of the Cross.

Leader: In the Name of the Father and of the Son and of the Holy Spirit. Amen.

All: I believe in God, the Father almighty, Creator of heaven and earth, and in Jesus Christ, his only Son, our Lord, who was conceived by the Holy Spirit, born of the Virgin Mary, suffered under Pontius Pilate, was crucified, died and was buried; he descended into hell; on the third day he rose again from the dead; he ascended into heaven, and is seated at the right hand of God the Father almighty; from there he will come to judge the living and the dead. I believe in the Holy Spirit, the holy catholic Church, the communion of saints, the forgiveness of sins, the resurrection of the body, and life everlasting. Amen.

On the bead closest to the Crucifix, pray the Our Father (the Lord's Prayer):

Leader: Our Father, who art in heaven, hallowed be thy name; thy kingdom come, thy will be done on earth, as it is in heaven.

All: Give us this day, our daily bread, and forgive us our trespasses, as we forgive those who trespass against us; and lead us not into temptation, but deliver us from evil. Amen.

On the next three beads, pray the Hail Mary:

Leader: Hail Mary, full of grace, the Lord is with thee; blessed art thou among women, and blessed is the fruit of thy womb, Jesus.

All: Holy Mary, Mother of God, pray for us sinners now, and at the hour of our death. Amen.

Then pray the Glory Be:

Leader: Glory be to the Father, and to the Son, and to the Holy Spirit,

All: as it was in the beginning, is now, and ever shall be, world without end. Amen.

Leader: Please turn your books to page____.

Parts of the Rosary

The Joyful Mysteries

Leader:

The First Joyful Mystery: The Annunciation of the Lord
Mary receives and conceives the Word of the Lord in her Heart, and conceives the Word in her womb by the overshadowing of the Holy Spirit.
"Behold the handmaid of the Lord; be it done to me according to thy word" (*Lk. 1:38, Douay Rheims*).
(Pause)
Our Father...ten Hail Marys...Glory be...
O my Jesus, forgive us our sins, save us from the fires of hell; lead all souls to Heaven, especially those in most need of Thy mercy and receptivity to Thy Divine Word.

The Second Joyful Mystery: The Visitation of Mary to Elizabeth
Mary receives the inspired Word of Elizabeth into her Heart, and from her Heart she says,
"My soul magnifies the Lord, and my spirit rejoices in God my Savior" *(Lk. 1:46-47).*
(Pause)
Our Father...ten Hail Marys...Glory be...
O my Jesus...in most need of Thy mercy and love of neighbor.

The Third Joyful Mystery: The Birth of Jesus
In her Heart Mary contemplates the newborn Savior and adores Him with her whole being as she
"wrapped Him in swaddling clothes, and laid Him in a manger..." *(Lk. 2:7).*
(Pause)
Our Father... ten Hail Marys...Glory be...
O my Jesus...in most need of Thy mercy and poverty of spirit.

The Fourth Joyful Mystery: The Presentation of the Child Jesus in the Temple
Mary's Heart is pierced by the sword of our sins, which pierced the Heart of Jesus on the Cross, so

"that thoughts out of many hearts may be revealed" *(Lk. 2:35)*.
(Pause)
Our Father…ten Hail Marys…Glory be…
O my Jesus…in most need of Thy mercy and fulfilling the Sunday obligation.

The Fifth Joyful Mystery: The Finding of the Child Jesus in the Temple
"And he went down with them and came to Nazareth, and was obedient to them; and his mother kept all these things in her Heart" *(Lk. 2:51)*.
(Pause)
Our Father… ten Hail Marys… Glory be…
O my Jesus…in most need of Thy mercy and obedience.

After leading 5 decades, please go to page 22 for the closing prayers "Hail Holy Queen" and the prayer introduced by "Let us pray."

The Luminous Mysteries

Leader:

The First Luminous Mystery: The Baptism of Our Lord
Jesus shows His humble Heart by accepting Baptism so that He would prepare the way for our Baptism with water and the Spirit. A voice from Heaven said,
"This is my beloved Son, with whom I am well pleased" *(Mt. 3:17)*.
(Pause)
Our Father… ten Hail Marys…Glory be…
O my Jesus, forgive us our sins, save us from the fires of hell; lead all souls to Heaven, especially those in most need of Thy mercy and the renewal of their baptismal promises.

The Second Luminous Mystery: The Marriage Feast at Cana
The Heart of Mary is moved with compassion for a married couple and those who did not believe.
"…the mother of Jesus said to Him, 'They have no wine'" *(Jn. 2:3)*.
(Pause)
Our Father… ten Hail Marys…Glory be…
O my Jesus…in most need of Thy mercy and the grace of commitment.

The Third Luminous Mystery: The Proclamation of the Gospel

18

Mary ponders the message of her Son in her Heart. Jesus said,
"...the kingdom of God is at hand; repent and believe in the gospel" *(Mk. 1:15)*.
(Pause)
Our Father... ten Hail Marys...Glory be...
O my Jesus...in most need of Thy mercy and conversion.

The Fourth Luminous Mystery: The Transfiguration of Jesus Christ

From the love of His Heart, Jesus reveals Himself in a foretaste of His Resurrection and offers a glimpse of His glory to be seen in the Beatific Vision.
"....a voice from the cloud said, 'This is my beloved Son, with whom I am well pleased; listen to Him'" *(Mt. 17:5)*.
(Pause)
Our Father... ten Hail Marys...Glory be...
O my Jesus...in most need of Thy mercy and truth.

The Fifth Luminous Mystery: The Institution of the Holy Eucharist

The Eucharist is the greatest Gift of the loving and merciful Heart of Jesus. This same Heart is truly present in the Eucharist to Whom we offer Mary's Heart.
"Let a man examine himself, and so eat of the bread and drink of the cup" *(I Cor. 11:28)*.
(Pause)
Our Father... ten Hail Marys...Glory be...
O my Jesus...in most need of Thy mercy and reverence for the Holy Eucharist.

After leading 5 decades, please go to page 22 for the closing prayers "Hail Holy Queen" and the prayer introduced by "Let us pray."

After leading 5 decades, please go to page 22

The Sorrowful Mysteries

Leader:

The First Sorrowful Mystery: The Agony of Jesus in the Garden

Mary joins her Heart to the Heart of her Son. In His prayer, Jesus reaffirms the unity of His Heart with the Father in saying,
"My Father, if it be possible, let this chalice pass from me; nevertheless, not as I will, but as Thou wilt" *(Mt. 26:39)*.

(Pause)

Our Father... ten Hail Marys...Glory be...

O my Jesus, forgive us our sins, save us from the fires of hell; lead all souls to Heaven, especially those in most need of Thy mercy and conformity to the will of God.

The Second Sorrowful Mystery: The Scourging of Jesus at the Pillar

Mary suffers the terrible scourging of her Son in her Heart in reparation for the sins of the flesh.

"By His wounds you have been healed" *(I Pet. 2:24)*.

(Pause)

Our Father... ten Hail Marys...Glory be...

O my Jesus...in most need of Thy mercy and mortification of the senses.

The Third Sorrowful Mystery: The Crowning of Jesus with Thorns

In witnessing the treatment of her Son, Mary's Heart is pierced with the thorns of His humiliation and rejection.

"And kneeling before him they mocked him, saying, 'Hail, King of the Jews!' And they spat upon him, and took the reed and struck him on the head" *(Mt. 27:29-30)*.

(Pause)

Our Father... ten Hail Marys...Glory be...

O my Jesus...in most need of Thy mercy and humility.

The Fourth Sorrowful Mystery: Jesus Carries the Cross

Following her Son, Mary patiently embraces the Cross in her Heart.

"And there followed Him a great multitude of the people, and of women who bewailed and lamented Him" *(Lk. 23:27)*.

(Pause)

Our Father... ten Hail Marys...Glory be...

O my Jesus...in most need of Thy mercy and patience.

The Fifth Sorrowful Mystery: The Crucifixion and Death of Our Lord

Mary suffers in her Heart and even body as Jesus suffers in His Heart and Body.

"When Jesus saw His mother, and the disciple whom He loved standing near, He said to His mother, 'Woman, behold, your son!' Then He said to the disciple, 'Behold, your mother!'" *(Jn. 19:26-27)*.

(Pause)

Our Father... ten Hail Marys...Glory be...

O my Jesus…in most need of Thy mercy and entrustment to the Heart of Mary.

After leading 5 decades, please go to page 22 for the closing prayers "Hail Holy Queen" and the prayer introduced by "Let us pray."

The Glorious Mysteries

Leader:

The First Glorious Mystery: The Resurrection of Jesus from the Dead

The Immaculate Heart of Mary is filled with joy over the Resurrection of her Son.

"Jesus came and stood among them and said to them, 'Peace be with you.'…And when He had said this, He breathed on them, and said to them, 'Receive the Holy Spirit. If you forgive the sins of any, they are forgiven; if you retain the sins of any, they are retained'" *(Jn. 20:19-23)*.
(Pause)
Our Father… ten Hail Marys…Glory be…
O my Jesus, forgive us our sins, save us from the fires of hell; lead all souls to Heaven, especially those in most need of Thy mercy and faith in You Jesus Christ.

The Second Glorious Mystery: The Ascension of Jesus into Heaven

The Heart of Mary rejoices at the Ascension of Jesus to the right hand of the Father, and yet her Heart yearns to be with her Son.
"While He blessed them, He parted from them, and was carried up into Heaven. And they worshipped Him…" *(Lk. 24:51-52)*.
(Pause)
Our Father… ten Hail Marys…Glory be…
O my Jesus…in most need of Thy mercy and Hope in You Jesus Christ.

The Third Glorious Mystery: The Descent of the Holy Spirit upon Mary and the Apostles

The Heart of Mary obtains from the Heart of Jesus that the graces of the Holy Spirit fill the hearts of the Apostles and those who form the Church.
"And there appeared to them tongues as of fire, distributed and resting on each one of them. And they were all filled with the Holy Spirit…" *(Acts 2:3-4)*.

(Pause)
Our Father... ten Hail Marys...Glory be...
O my Jesus...in most need of Thy mercy and the gifts of the Holy Spirit.

The Fourth Glorious Mystery: The Assumption of Mary into Heaven
Jesus draws His Mother, body and soul, into Heaven. And so the Heart of Mary is joined to the Heart of Jesus in beholding the beatific vision.
"Then God's temple in heaven was opened, and the ark of his covenant was seen within His temple..." *(Rev. 11:19)*.
(Pause)
Our Father... ten Hail Marys...Glory be...
O my Jesus...in most need of Thy mercy and salvation.

The Fifth Glorious Mystery: The Crowning of Mary as Queen of Heaven and Earth
Jesus is the King of Mary's Heart and our hearts also, while Mary is the Queen of Jesus' Heart and our hearts as well.
"And a great sign appeared in heaven, a woman clothed with the sun, with the moon under her feet, and on her head a crown of twelve stars..." *(Rev. 12:1)*.
(Pause)
Our Father... ten Hail Marys...Glory be...
O my Jesus...in most need of Thy mercy and the mediation of the Heart of Mary.

At the end of the five decades, say the Hail Holy Queen and the prayer introduced by "Let us pray."

All: Hail Holy Queen, Mother of mercy, our life, our sweetness and our hope. To thee do we cry, poor banished children of Eve. To thee do we send up our sighs, mourning and weeping in this vale of tears. Turn then most gracious advocate, thine eyes of mercy towards us, and after this our exile, show unto us the blessed fruit of thy womb, Jesus. O clement, O loving, O sweet Virgin Mary. Pray for us, O holy Mother of God. That we may be made worthy of the promises of Christ.

Leader: Let us pray.

All: O God, whose only begotten Son, by His Life, Death, and Resurrection, has purchased for us the rewards of eternal life, grant we beseech thee, that meditating on these mysteries of the Most Holy Rosary of the

Blessed Virgin Mary, we may imitate what they contain, and obtain what they promise, through the same Christ Our Lord. Amen.

Leader: For those who wish to receive the Brown Scapular, please make some time to prepare yourself first. *The Brown Scapular* pamphlet is available to help you prepare to receive the Scapular next month. Those who are prepared to receive the Scapular today may do so after the_____ *(prayers for the Holy Father or reception of the Pilgrim Virgin statue).*

Leader: Of great importance, for the love of Jesus, let us receive Him in Holy Communion with the intention of making reparation to the Immaculate Heart of Mary. *(Pause)*

Leader: For the Communion of reparation, you could turn to the top of page 26 for some helpful prayers to meditate on after you receive Holy Communion.

2). The Holy Mass and Communion *with the intention of making reparation to the Immaculate Heart of Mary*

General Intercessions

With the approval of the pastor, the Communal First Saturdays leaders may select at least a few of the following petitions to be read for the General Intercessions during Mass by simply selecting the petition numbers.

Priest or Leader:

For the needs of the Church

1. That we may advance in gratitude to our Creator and Redeemer, especially for the Gift of Himself in the Holy Eucharist and in His Word together with the Gift of His Mother. *All: Lord hear our prayer.*

2. That reparation be made to the Immaculate Heart of Mary for the offenses against the Immaculate Conception, her Perpetual Virginity, her Motherhood of God and mankind, her place in children's hearts, and her Sacred Images. Let us pray to the Lord. *Lord hear our prayer.*

3. That You Lord, please receive the suffering of all humanity in all times in reparation to the Hearts of Jesus and Mary. Let us pray to the Lord. *Lord hear our prayer.*

4. For the Holy Father and that he may give a new impetus to the First Saturdays Liturgy and devotion of reparation. Let us pray to the Lord. *Lord hear our prayer.*

5. For the conversion of Russia, and the reunion of the Catholic Church and the Eastern churches. Let us pray to the Lord. *Lord hear our prayer.*

6. For the sanctification of all bishops and priests. Let us pray to the Lord. *Lord hear our prayer.*

7. That the Church in *(name of country)* may do its part for the greater sanctification of the Universal Church with the help of the First Saturdays, so that she may be prepared for reunion with the other separated churches. Let us pray to the Lord. *Lord hear our prayer.*

8. For those graces which will help priests to be good confessors and which will help penitents to make good confessions. Let us pray to the Lord. *Lord hear our prayer.*

9. For the beatification of the Servant of God, Sr. Lucia, and in thanksgiving for the canonizations of Blessed Jacinta and Blessed Francisco. Let us pray to the Lord. *Lord hear our prayer.*

For public authorities and the salvation of the world

10. That through the First Saturdays, many souls may be saved from the eternal suffering of Hell. Let us pray to the Lord. *Lord hear our prayer.*

11. That we may take part in spreading the First Saturdays throughout the world by the Divine Fire, and for new apostles to carry out this work. Let us pray to the Lord. *Lord hear our prayer.*

12. That we may join with the Church in entrusting those children who have died without the rite of Baptism to the mercy of God. Let us pray to the Lord. *Lord hear our prayer.*

13. That the Jewish people may acknowledge the fulfillment of their religion in Jesus the Messiah and His Kingdom, and that all peoples on earth may come into the fullness of Faith in the Son of God. Let us pray to the Lord. *Lord hear our prayer.*

14. For the conversion of the Muslim people. Let us pray to the Lord. *Lord hear our prayer.*

15. That political leaders may be guided by the light of Christ rather than vested interests. Let us pray to the Lord. *Lord hear our prayer.*

For those oppressed by any need

16. That the laws of the nations may be founded upon the natural law, and that all nations may recognize the right to life from conception, and freedom of religion. Let us pray to the Lord. *Lord hear our prayer.*

17. For conscience rights and religious liberty; that all people of good will may work together against threats to these fundamental rights (*USCCB*). Let us pray to the Lord. *Lord hear our prayer.*

18. For the healing of victims of abuse and for the repentance of their perpetrators. Let us pray to the Lord. *Lord hear our prayer.*

19. For the sanctification and restoration of families. Let us pray to the Lord. *Lord hear our prayer.*

20. For the mothers and fathers of aborted children as well as those who have encouraged these acts. Let us pray to the Lord. *Lord hear our prayer.*

21. For the doctors and medical personnel who have participated in abortion. Let us pray to the Lord. *Lord hear our prayer.*

22. For the souls in Purgatory. Let us pray to the Lord. *Lord hear our prayer.*

The priest may add other petitions.

The Communion of Reparation

After receiving Holy Communion it is suggested that one meditate privately on the following Fatima prayers or words to that effect:

Most Holy Trinity, Father, Son, and Holy Spirit I adore You profoundly. I offer You the Most Precious Body, Blood, Soul, and Divinity of Jesus Christ, present in all the tabernacles throughout the world, in reparation for the outrages, sacrileges, and indifference by which He is offended. And through the infinite merits of His most Sacred Heart, and of the Immaculate Heart of Mary, I beg the conversion of poor sinners.

O Most Holy Trinity, I adore You. My God, my God, I love You in the most Blessed Sacrament.

O Jesus, this is for love of You, for the conversion of sinners, for the Holy Father, and in reparation for the sins committed against the Immaculate Heart of Mary. *(Jacinta added "the Holy Father.")*

3). Meditation *with the intention of making reparation to the Immaculate Heart of Mary*

Introduction to the Meditation

In keeping Our Lady company for 15 minutes while meditating on the mysteries of the Rosary with the intention of making reparation to her Immaculate Heart, we provide a way of doing so with an adapted communal form of lectio divina.

Communal Scripture Meditation
(after Holy Mass)

Note to Leaders:
Before leading the Scripture Meditation, please be sure to read Appendix F as well as the information regarding the Meditation in Appendix G of "The Communal First Saturdays" book.

*Please only read text that is not italicized and is not a heading. Please note that when a pause is indicated, it is approximately 5 seconds or more, and when a long pause is indicated, it is approximately **20 seconds** or more. There should be some way of keeping track of time such as with a digital clock.*

The Scripture Meditation itself should take at least 15 minutes. Yet, it may not be necessary to read all the Scripture verses to reach 15 minutes. The total time the leader is normally up at the lectern is 20 minutes, which gives sufficient time for the introductory instructions, the meditation, as well as the other steps of the lectio divina.

Leader: The meditation will begin in a moment for those who wish to complete the First Saturdays in a communal form. You will need a copy of the books found at the _____. Before leaving, please return them. Please turn to page 27 to follow along.

Leader:

- Now in praise and thanksgiving to the Father for His Son present within us in the Holy Eucharist and by the grace of the Holy Spirit, we will keep **Our Lady company for 15 minutes** while **meditating** on at least two mysteries of the Rosary, in an adapted form of *lectio divina*, with the **intention of making reparation to her Immaculate Heart**. *(Pause)*

- Before and after reading one or more Scripture verses, I will ask a question. *(Pause)* These questions will be announced out loud three separate times to help us learn. Otherwise, we should ask them silently after each Scripture reading.

-

- As in Acts 8 where Philip guided the eunuch in understanding the Scripture, how much more can Our Blessed Mother guide us in understanding the Scripture? With each reading, we will ask Our Blessed Mother, who is full of the Holy Spirit, to help us understand the Scripture.

- Pope Benedict XVI confirmed this approach by saying, "Let us now allow her, our mother and teacher, to guide us in reflecting on the Word of God that we have just heard" *(October 19, 2008)*.

- Our meditation will now begin… (*15 minutes should begin now*)

Leader: Hail Mary, full of grace, obtain for us the grace of the Holy Spirit to grasp the meaning of the Word of God and be transformed by it. *(Short pause.)* Above all, help us to be aware that we have just received your Son in Holy Communion and that by Holy Communion He dwells within us as He dwelled in you at His Conception. In keeping you company, lead us to Jesus within, and please accept our meditation and ourselves in reparation for the sins which have offended your Immaculate Heart. *(Short pause.)*

Leader: Let us close our eyes and call to mind that we are in Our Lady's company. *(Pause).* Let Our Lady lead us to Jesus in the Holy Eucharist within us.

(Pause) (Pause from here forward equals approximately 5 seconds)

Leader: Let us first consider the following words of Scripture regarding the Child Jesus: "After three days they found him in the temple, sitting among the teachers, listening to them and asking them questions..." *(Lk. 2:46). (Pause)*

Leader: Please turn to page ___ for the meditation for the month of _____.

After the Scripture meditation, continue with the following:

Prayer

Leader: Now after meditating on the Scripture, "what do we say to the Lord in response to his word?" *(Verbum Domini).* Let us pray together with Our Lady:

All: "Behold the handmaid of the Lord; be it done to me according to thy word" *(Lk. 1:38, Douay Rheims).*

(Pause)

Leader: Let us pause to pray silently.

(Pause)

Here one may engage in petition, intercession, thanksgiving, and praise (cf. Verbum Domini).

Contemplation

In the light of our meditation and prayer we turn to contemplation. In contemplation, "we take up, as a gift from God, his own way of seeing and judging reality, and ask ourselves what conversion of mind, heart and life is the Lord asking of us?" (Verbum Domini).

Leader: Now we contemplate the following question in the light of our meditation on the mysteries of the Rosary: "what conversion of mind, heart and life is the Lord asking of us?" *(Verbum Domini).*

(Pause)

Leader: In Mary's company, let us silently turn our loving gaze to Jesus in the midst of the Father and the Holy Spirit dwelling within us.

(Long pause)

In other words, we gaze upon the Holy Trinity dwelling within us. .

Action

"We do well also to remember that the process of lectio divina is not concluded until it arrives at action (actio), which moves the believer to make his or her life a gift for others in charity" (Verbum Domini). Let us then imitate Our Lady:

Leader: Now let us imitate the action of Our Lady after receiving the Word made Flesh. As together we say:

Leader: "In those days Mary arose and went with haste into the hill country…" *(Lk. 1:39).*

(short pause)

Leader: Also let us say together:

All: We make our "life a gift for others in charity" *(Verbum Domini).*

(Pause)

Leader: This concludes our communal meditation in Our Lady's company.

Leader: We will now pray the Litany of the Blessed Virgin Mary on page 30.

       As an extra gift to Our Lady, it is recommended that one pray the Litany of the Blessed Virgin Mary.

2.25 The Litany of the Blessed Virgin Mary (The Litany of Loreto)

Leader: Let us invoke Our Lady in praise and thanksgiving for inviting us to keep her company during our meditation on the mysteries of the Rosary.

Lord, have mercy on us. *All: Christ have mercy on us.*
Lord, have mercy on us. Christ, hear us. *All: Christ graciously hear us.*
God, the Father of Heaven, *All: have mercy on us.*
God the Son, Redeemer of the world, *All: have mercy on us.*
God the Holy Spirit, *All: have mercy on us.*
Holy Trinity, one God, *All: have mercy on us.*
Holy Mary, *All: pray for us.*
Holy Mother of God, *[etc.]*
Holy Virgin of virgins,
Mother of Christ,
Mother of the Church,
Mother of divine grace,
Mother most pure,
Mother most chaste,
Mother inviolate,
Mother most amiable,
Mother most admirable,
Mother of good counsel,
Mother of our Creator,
Mother of our Savior,
Virgin most prudent,
Virgin most venerable,
Virgin most renowned,
Virgin most powerful,
Virgin most merciful,
Virgin most faithful,
Mirror of justice,

Seat of wisdom,
Cause of our joy,
Spiritual vessel,
Vessel of honor,
Singular vessel of devotion,
Mystical rose,
Tower of David,
Tower of ivory,
House of gold,
Ark of the covenant,
Gate of Heaven,
Morning star,
Health of the sick,
Refuge of sinners,
Comforter of the afflicted,
Help of Christians,
Queen of Angels,
Queen of Patriarchs,
Queen of Prophets,
Queen of Apostles,
Queen of Martyrs,
Queen of Confessors,
Queen of Virgins,
Queen of all Saints,
Queen conceived without original sin,
Queen assumed into Heaven,
Queen of the most holy Rosary,
Queen of families,
Queen of Peace,

Lamb of God, Who takes away the sins of the world,
All: spare us, O Lord.
Lamb of God, Who takes away the sins of the world,
All: graciously hear us, O Lord.
Lamb of God, Who takes away the sins of the world,
All: have mercy on us.

Pray for us, O holy Mother of God. *All: That we may be made worthy of the promises of Christ.*

Let us pray. *All:* Grant, unto us Thy servants, we beseech Thee, O Lord God, at all times to enjoy health of soul and body; and, by the glorious intercession of Blessed Mary ever Virgin, when freed from the sorrows of this present life, to enter into that joy which hath no end. Through Christ our Lord. Amen.

2.26 Intention to Gain any Indulgences and Prayers for the Intentions of the Holy Father

Following the Litany of the Blessed Virgin Mary, the leader then closes the Communal First Saturdays with the prayers for the Holy Father. These prayers will satisfy for one of the conditions of gaining a plenary indulgence.

Leader: Let us make the intention to gain any indulgences granted by the Church for ourselves and the souls in Purgatory.

Leader: Let us pray for the intentions of the Holy Father.

All:

Our Father...
Hail Mary...
Glory Be...

After the prayers for the Holy Father or after the reception of the Pilgrim Virgin statue, the faithful who have not previously received the Brown Scapular may receive it with the approval of the pastor. While the Communal First Saturdays can be conducted without the reception of the Brown Scapular, we should remember that Sr. Lucia said that the Rosary and the Scapular are inseparable.

Note for the Leader:

The leader will now close the Communal First Saturdays devotion with a few appropriate words and invite those who wish to receive the Brown Scapular to come to the designated area (go to Appendix II). Any important announcements can also be made such as a reminder of the next Communal First Saturdays.

Or

The leader will say the following if the parish has the reception of the Pilgrim Virgin statue in the church after the Communal First Saturdays.

Leader: Now, we will have the reception of the Pilgrim Virgin statue with a reenactment of the mystery of the Visitation. As we just heard, the action step after the *lectio divina* is to go out and perform a work of charity. After receiving the Word made Flesh, Mary did this by going in haste to the hill country to visit her elderly cousin who was with child *(Go to Appendix I).*

2.27 Reception of the Brown Scapular

Leaders should consult Appendix II for information regarding the bestowal of blessed Brown Scapulars (cf. also "The Communal First Saturdays" book, Part II, Section One, Ch. 2, q. 39).

2.3 *Monthly Meditations on the Mysteries of the Rosary*

January

Communal Scripture Meditation as Lectio Divina

Leader: To harmonize with the liturgical season of Christmas, we will now meditate on the 3rd Joyful Mystery, the Birth of Jesus, beginning with Mt. 1:18.

(Pause)

Reading

Leader: O Blessed Mother, what does this Scripture say? *(basado en Verbum Domini, Pope Benedict XVI)*

18 Now this is how the birth of Jesus Christ came about. When his mother Mary was betrothed to Joseph, but before they lived together, she was found with child through the holy Spirit.
19 Joseph her husband, since he was a righteous man, yet unwilling to expose her to shame, decided to divorce her quietly.

33

(Pause)

Meditation

Leader: O Blessed Mother, what does this Scripture say to us, personally? *(based on Verbum Domini)*

(Long pause) (a long pause equals approximately 20 seconds)

Reading

Leader: O Blessed Mother, what does this Scripture say?

20 Such was his intention when, behold, the angel of the Lord appeared to him in a dream and said, "Joseph, son of David, do not be afraid to take Mary your wife into your home. For it is through the holy Spirit that this child has been conceived in her.
21 She will bear a son and you are to name him Jesus, because he will save his people from their sins."

(Pause)

Meditation

Leader: O Blessed Mother, what does this Scripture say to us, personally?

(Long pause)

Reading and Meditation

The leader will continue reading Scripture verses and pausing, without asking questions, until the next mystery. The faithful may continue to ask themselves the two questions silently after each Scripture reading.

22 All this took place to fulfill what the Lord had said through the prophet:
23 "Behold, the virgin shall be with child and bear a son, and they shall name him Emmanuel," which means "God is with us."
24 When Joseph awoke, he did as the angel of the Lord had commanded him and took his wife into his home. *(Long pause)*

After each reading, silently ask:
O Blessed Mother, what does this Scripture say?
O Blessed Mother, what does this Scripture say to me, personally?

Leader: We now continue with passages from Mt. 2.

1 When Jesus was born in Bethlehem of Judea, in the days of King Herod, behold, magi from the east arrived in Jerusalem,
2 saying, "Where is the newborn king of the Jews? We saw his star at its rising and have come to do him homage." *(Long pause)*

3 When King Herod heard this, he was greatly troubled, and all Jerusalem with him.
4 Assembling all the chief priests and the scribes of the people, he inquired of them where the Messiah was to be born. *(Long pause)*

5 They said to him, "In Bethlehem of Judea, for thus it has been written through the prophet:
6 And you, Bethlehem, land of Judah,
are by no means least among the rulers of Judah;
since from you shall come a ruler,
who is to shepherd my people Israel.'" *(Long pause)*

7 Then Herod called the magi secretly and ascertained from them the time of the star's appearance.
8 He sent them to Bethlehem and said, "Go and search diligently for the child. When you have found him, bring me word, that I too may go and do him homage." *(Long pause)*

9 After their audience with the king they set out. And behold, the star that they had seen at its rising preceded them, until it came and stopped over the place where the child was.
10 They were overjoyed at seeing the star, *(Long pause)*

11 and on entering the house they saw the child with Mary his mother. They prostrated themselves and did him homage. Then they opened their treasures and offered him gifts of gold, frankincense, and myrrh. *(Long pause)*

12 And having been warned in a dream not to return to Herod, they departed fo their country by another way.

13 When they had departed, behold, the angel of the Lord appeared to Joseph in dream and said, "Rise, take the child and his mother, flee to Egypt, and stay there until I tell you. Herod is going to search for the child to destroy him." *(Long pause)*

14 Joseph rose and took the child and his mother by night and departed fo Egypt.

15 He stayed there until the death of Herod, that what the Lord had said through the prophet might be fulfilled, "Out of Egypt I called my son." *(Long pause)*

16 When Herod realized that he had been deceived by the magi, he became furious. He ordered the massacre of all the boys in Bethlehem and its vicinity two years old and under, in accordance with the time he had ascertained from the magi. *(Long pause)*

17 Then was fulfilled what had been said through Jeremiah the prophet:

18 "A voice was heard in Ramah, sobbing and loud lamentation; Rachel weeping for her children, and she would not be consoled, since they were no more." *(Long pause)*

Leader: In harmony with the liturgical feast we celebrate this month, we will now meditate on the 1st Luminous Mystery, the Baptism of Our Lord beginning with Mt. 3:13.

(Pause)

Reading

Leader: O Blessed Mother, what does this Scripture say?

13 Then Jesus came from Galilee to John at the Jordan to be baptized by him.

(Pause)

Meditation

Leader: O Blessed Mother, what does this Scripture say to us, personally?

(Long pause)

Reading and Meditation

The leader will continue reading Scripture verses and pausing, without asking questions. The faithful may continue to ask themselves the two questions silently after each Scripture reading.

14 John tried to prevent him, saying, "I need to be baptized by you, and yet you are coming to me?" *(Long pause)*

15 Jesus said to him in reply, "Allow it now, for thus it is fitting for us to fulfill all righteousness." Then he allowed him. *(Long pause)*

16 After Jesus was baptized, he came up from the water and behold, the heavens were opened [for him], and he saw the Spirit of God descending like a dove [and] coming upon him. *(Long pause)*

17 And a voice came from the heavens, saying, "This is my beloved Son, with whom I am well pleased." *(Long pause)*

At the end of 15 minutes, say:

Leader: To continue, please turn to "Prayer" on page 28 in your book.

February

Communal Scripture Meditation as Lectio Divina

Leader: In harmony with the liturgical feast, we will now meditate on the 4th Joyful Mystery, the Presentation of the Child Jesus in the Temple, beginning with Lk. 2:22.

(Pause)

Reading

Leader: O Blessed Mother, what does this Scripture say? *(basado en Verbum Domini, Pope Benedict XVI)*

22 When the days were completed for their purification according to the law of Moses, they took him up to Jerusalem to present him to the Lord,

(Pause)

Meditation

Leader: O Blessed Mother, what does this Scripture say to us, personally? *(based on Verbum Domini)*

(Long pause) (a long pause equals approximately 20 seconds)

Reading

Leader: O Blessed Mother, what does this Scripture say?

23 just as it is written in the law of the Lord, "Every male that opens the womb shall be consecrated to the Lord,"

(Pause)

Meditation

Leader: O Blessed Mother, what does this Scripture say to us, personally?

(Long pause)

Reading and Meditation

The leader will continue reading Scripture verses and pausing, without asking questions, until the next mystery. The faithful may continue to ask themselves the two questions silently after each Scripture reading.

24 and to offer the sacrifice of "a pair of turtledoves or two young pigeons," in accordance with the dictate in the law of the Lord. *(Long pause)*

After each reading, silently ask:

O Blessed Mother, what does this Scripture say?
O Blessed Mother, what does this Scripture say to me, personally?

25 Now there was a man in Jerusalem whose name was Simeon. This man was righteous and devout, awaiting the consolation of Israel, and the holy Spirit was upon him.
26 It had been revealed to him by the holy Spirit that he should not see death before he had seen the Messiah of the Lord. *(Long pause)*

27 He came in the Spirit into the temple; and when the parents brought in the child Jesus to perform the custom of the law in regard to him,
28 he took him into his arms and blessed God, saying:
29 "Now, Master, you may let your servant go in peace, according to your word, *(Long pause)*

30 for my eyes have seen your salvation,
31 which you prepared in sight of all the peoples,
32 a light for revelation to the Gentiles, and glory for your people Israel." *(Long pause)*

33 The child's father and mother were amazed at what was said about him;
34 and Simeon blessed them and said to Mary his mother, "Behold, this child is destined for the fall and rise of many in Israel, and to be a sign that will be contradicted *(Long pause)*

35 (and you yourself a sword will pierce) so that the thoughts of many hearts may be revealed." *(Long pause)*

36 There was also a prophetess, Anna, the daughter of Phanuel, of the tribe of Asher. She was advanced in years, having lived seven years with her husband after her marriage,
37 and then as a widow until she was eighty-four. She never left the temple, but worshiped night and day with fasting and prayer. *(Long pause)*

38 And coming forward at that very time, she gave thanks to God and spoke about the child to all who were awaiting the redemption of Jerusalem. *(Long pause)*

39 When they had fulfilled all the prescriptions of the law of the Lord, they returned to Galilee, to their own town of Nazareth.

40 The child grew and became strong, filled with wisdom; and the favor of God was upon him. *(Long pause)*

Leader: We will now meditate on the 5ᵗʰ Joyful Mystery, the Finding of the Child Jesus in the Temple, beginning with Lk. 2:41

.

(Pause)

Reading

Leader: O Blessed Mother, what does this Scripture say?

41 Each year his parents went to Jerusalem for the feast of Passover,
42 and when he was twelve years old, they went up according to festival custom.
43 After they had completed its days, as they were returning, the boy Jesus remained behind in Jerusalem, but his parents did not know it.

(Pause)

Meditation

Leader: O Blessed Mother, what does this Scripture say to us, personally?

(Long pause)

Reading and Meditation

The leader will continue reading Scripture verses and pausing, without asking questions. The faithful may continue to ask themselves the two questions silently after each Scripture reading.

44 Thinking that he was in the caravan, they journeyed for a day and looked for him among their relatives and acquaintances,
45 but not finding him, they returned to Jerusalem to look for him. *(Long pause)*

46 After three days they found him in the temple, sitting in the midst of the teachers, listening to them and asking them questions,
47 and all who heard him were astounded at his understanding and his answers. *(Long pause)*

48 When his parents saw him, they were astonished, and his mother said to him, 'Son, why have you done this to us? Your father and I have been looking for you with great anxiety." *(Long pause)*

49 And he said to them, "Why were you looking for me? Did you not know that I must be in my Father's house?"
50 But they did not understand what he said to them. *(Long pause)*

51 He went down with them and came to Nazareth, and was obedient to them; and his mother kept all these things in her heart.
52 And Jesus advanced (in) wisdom and age and favor before God and man. *(Long pause)*

Leader: We now continue with passages from Wisdom 7.

8 I preferred her to scepters and thrones, and I accounted wealth as nothing in comparison with her. 9 Neither did I liken to her any priceless gem, because all gold is but a little sand in her sight, and silver will be accounted as clay before her. *(Long pause)*

10 I loved her more than health and beauty, and I chose to have her rather than light, because her radiance never ceases. 11 All good things came to me along with her, and in her hands uncounted wealth. *(Long pause)*

12 I rejoiced in them all, because wisdom leads them; but I did not know that she was their mother. *(Long pause)*

13 I learned without guile and I impart without grudging; I do not hide her wealth, 14 for it is an unfailing treasure for men; those who get it obtain friendship with God, commended for the gifts that come from instruction. *(Long pause)*

At the end of 15 minutes, say:

Leader: To continue, please turn to "Prayer" on page 28 in your book.

March (A)

Communal Scripture Meditation as Lectio Divina

If the Feast of the Annunciation is celebrated in March, then use thi meditation. Otherwise, use March (B).

Leader: In anticipation of the liturgical solemnity we will celebrate this month we will now meditate on the 1st Joyful Mystery, the Annunciation of the Lord, beginning with Lk. 1:26.

(Pause)

Reading

Leader: O Blessed Mother, what does this Scripture say? *(basado en Verbum Domini, Pope Benedict XVI)*

26 In the sixth month, the angel Gabriel was sent from God to a town of Galilee called Nazareth,
27 to a virgin betrothed to a man named Joseph, of the house of David, and the virgin's name was Mary.

(Pause)

Meditation

Leader: O Blessed Mother, what does this Scripture say to us, personally? *(based on Verbum Domini)*

(Long pause) (a long pause equals approximately 20 seconds)

Reading

Leader: O Blessed Mother, what does this Scripture say?

28 And coming to her, he said, "Hail, favored one [full of grace]! The Lord is with you." *(Brackets are ours)*
29 But she was greatly troubled at what was said and pondered what sort of greeting this might be.

(Pause)

Meditation

Leader: O Blessed Mother, what does this Scripture say to us, personally?

(Long pause)

Reading and Meditation

The leader will continue reading Scripture verses and pausing, without asking questions, until the next mystery. The faithful may continue to ask themselves the two questions silently after each Scripture reading.

30 Then the angel said to her, "Do not be afraid, Mary, for you have found favor with God.
31 Behold, you will conceive in your womb and bear a son, and you shall name him Jesus. *(Long pause)*

After each reading, silently ask:
O Blessed Mother, what does this Scripture say?
O Blessed Mother, what does this Scripture say to me, personally?

32 He will be great and will be called Son of the Most High, and the Lord God will give him the throne of David his father,
33 and he will rule over the house of Jacob forever, and of his kingdom there will be no end." *(Long pause)*

34 But Mary said to the angel, "How can this be, since I have no relations with a man?"
35 And the angel said to her in reply, "The holy Spirit will come upon you, and the power of the Most High will overshadow you. Therefore the child to be born will be called holy, the Son of God. *(Long pause)*

36 And behold, Elizabeth, your relative, has also conceived a son in her old age, and this is the sixth month for her who was called barren;
37 for nothing will be impossible for God." *(Long pause)*

38 Mary said, "Behold, I am the handmaid of the Lord. May it be done to me according to your word." Then the angel departed from her. *(Long pause)*

Leader: To harmonize with the liturgical season of Lent, we will now meditate on the 1st Sorrowful Mystery, the Agony of Jesus in the Garden, beginning with Mt. 26:36.

(Pause)

Reading

Leader: O Blessed Mother, what does this Scripture say?

[36] Then Jesus went with them to a place called Gethsem'ane, and he said to his disciples, "Sit here, while I go yonder and pray." [37] And taking with him Peter and the two sons of Zeb'edee, he began to be sorrowful and troubled.

(Pause)

Meditation

Leader: O Blessed Mother, what does this Scripture say to us, personally?

(Long pause)

Reading and Meditation

The leader will continue reading Scripture verses and pausing, without asking questions. The faithful may continue to ask themselves the two questions silently after each Scripture reading.

[38] Then he said to them, "My soul is very sorrowful, even to death; remain here, and watch with me." [39] And going a little farther he fell on his face and prayed, "My Father, if it be possible, let this cup pass from me; nevertheless, not as I will, but as thou wilt." *(Long pause)*

[40] And he came to the disciples and found them sleeping; and he said to Peter, "So, could you not watch with me one hour? [41] Watch and pray that you may not enter into temptation; the spirit indeed is willing, but the flesh is weak." *(Long pause)*

[42] Again, for the second time, he went away and prayed, "My Father, if this cannot pass unless I drink it, thy will be done." [43] And again he came and found them sleeping, for their eyes were heavy. [44] So, leaving them again, he went away and prayed for the third time, saying the same words. *(Long pause)*

[45] Then he came to the disciples and said to them, "Are you still sleeping and taking your rest? Behold, the hour is at hand, and the Son of man is betrayed into the hands of sinners. [46] Rise, let us be going; see, my betrayer is at hand." *(Long pause)*

[47] While he was still speaking, Judas came, one of the twelve, and with him a great crowd with swords and clubs, from the chief priests and the elders of the people. [48] Now the betrayer had given them a sign, saying, "The one I shall kiss is the man; seize him." *(Long pause)*

[49] And he came up to Jesus at once and said, "Hail, Master!" And he kissed him. [50] Jesus said to him, "Friend, why are you here?" Then they came up and laid hands on Jesus and seized him. *(Long pause)*

[51] And behold, one of those who were with Jesus stretched out his hand and drew his sword, and struck the slave of the high priest, and cut off his ear. [52] Then Jesus said to him, "Put your sword back into its place; for all who take the sword will perish by the sword. *(Long pause)*

[53] Do you think that I cannot appeal to my Father, and he will at once send me more than twelve legions of angels? [54] But how then should the scriptures be fulfilled, that it must be so?" *(Long pause)*

[55] At that hour Jesus said to the crowds, "Have you come out as against a robber, with swords and clubs to capture me? Day after day I sat in the temple teaching, and you did not seize me. [56] But all this has taken place, that the scriptures of the prophets might be fulfilled." Then all the disciples forsook him and fled. *(Long pause)*

Leader: We will now meditate on the 2nd Sorrowful Mystery, the Scourging of Jesus at the Pillar, beginning with Mt. 27:24.

(Pause)

[24] So when Pilate saw that he was gaining nothing, but rather that a riot was beginning, he took water and washed his hands before the crowd, saying, "I am innocent of this righteous man's blood; see to it yourselves." *(Long pause)*

[25] And all the people answered, "His blood be on us and on our children!" [26] Then he released for them Barab′bas, and having scourged Jesus, delivered him to be crucified. *(Long pause)*

At the end of 15 minutes, say:

Leader: To continue, please turn to "Prayer" on page 28 in your book.

March (B)

Communal Scripture Meditation as Lectio Divina

If the Feast of the Annunciation is not celebrated in March, then use this meditation. Otherwise, use March (A).

Leader: To harmonize with the liturgical season of Lent, we will now meditate on the 1st Sorrowful Mystery, the Agony of Jesus in the Garden, beginning with Mt. 26:36.

(Pause)

Reading

Leader: O Blessed Mother, what does this Scripture say? *(basado en Verbum Domini, Pope Benedict XVI)*

[36] Then Jesus went with them to a place called Gethsem′ane, and he said to his disciples, "Sit here, while I go yonder and pray." [37] And taking with him Peter and the two sons of Zeb′edee, he began to be sorrowful and troubled.

(Pause)

Meditation

Leader: O Blessed Mother, what does this Scripture say to us, personally? *(based on Verbum Domini)*

(Long pause) (a long pause equals approximately 20 seconds)

Reading

Leader: O Blessed Mother, what does this Scripture say?

[38] Then he said to them, "My soul is very sorrowful, even to death; remain here, and watch with me." [39] And going a little farther he fell on his face and prayed, "My Father, if it be possible, let this cup pass from me; nevertheless, not as I will, but as thou wilt."

(Pause)

Meditation

Leader: O Blessed Mother, what does this Scripture say to us, personally?

(Long pause)

Reading and Meditation

The leader will continue reading Scripture verses and pausing, without asking questions, until the next mystery. The faithful may continue to ask themselves the two questions silently after each Scripture reading.

[40] And he came to the disciples and found them sleeping; and he said to Peter, "So, could you not watch with me one hour? [41] Watch and pray that you may not enter into temptation; the spirit indeed is willing, but the flesh is weak." *(Long pause)*

After each reading, silently ask:
O Blessed Mother, what does this Scripture say?
O Blessed Mother, what does this Scripture say to me, personally?

[42] Again, for the second time, he went away and prayed, "My Father, if this cannot pass unless I drink it, thy will be done." [43] And again he came and found them sleeping, for their eyes were heavy. [44] So, leaving them again, he went away and prayed for the third time, saying the same words. *(Long pause)*

[45] Then he came to the disciples and said to them, "Are you still sleeping and taking your rest? Behold, the hour is at hand, and the Son of man is betrayed into

the hands of sinners. [46] Rise, let us be going; see, my betrayer is at hand." *(Long pause)*

[47] While he was still speaking, Judas came, one of the twelve, and with him a great crowd with swords and clubs, from the chief priests and the elders of the people. [48] Now the betrayer had given them a sign, saying, "The one I shall kiss is the man; seize him." *(Long pause)*

[49] And he came up to Jesus at once and said, "Hail, Master!" And he kissed him. [50] Jesus said to him, "Friend, why are you here?" Then they came up and laid hands on Jesus and seized him. *(Long pause)*

[51] And behold, one of those who were with Jesus stretched out his hand and drew his sword, and struck the slave of the high priest, and cut off his ear. [52] Then Jesus said to him, "Put your sword back into its place; for all who take the sword will perish by the sword. *(Long pause)*

[53] Do you think that I cannot appeal to my Father, and he will at once send me more than twelve legions of angels? [54] But how then should the scriptures be fulfilled, that it must be so?" *(Long pause)*

[55] At that hour Jesus said to the crowds, "Have you come out as against a robber with swords and clubs to capture me? Day after day I sat in the temple teaching and you did not seize me. [56] But all this has taken place, that the scriptures of the prophets might be fulfilled." Then all the disciples forsook him and fled. *(Long pause)*

Leader: We will now meditate on the 2nd Sorrowful Mystery, the Scourging of Jesus at the Pillar, beginning with Mt. 27:24.

(Pause)

Reading

Leader: O Blessed Mother, what does this Scripture say?

[24] So when Pilate saw that he was gaining nothing, but rather that a riot was beginning, he took water and washed his hands before the crowd, saying, "I am innocent of this righteous man's blood; see to it yourselves."

(Pause)

Meditation

Leader: O Blessed Mother, what does this Scripture say to us, personally?

(Long pause)

Reading and Meditation

The leader will continue reading Scripture verses and pausing, without asking questions. The faithful may continue to ask themselves the two questions silently after each Scripture reading.

[25] And all the people answered, "His blood be on us and on our children!" [26] Then he released for them Barab′bas, and having scourged Jesus, delivered him to be crucified. *(Long pause)*

Leader: We now continue with passages from Is. 53.

53 Who has believed what we have heard? And to whom has the arm of the LORD been revealed?
[2] For he grew up before him like a young plant, and like a root out of dry ground; he had no form or comeliness that we should look at him, and no beauty that we should desire him. *(Long pause)*

[3] He was despised and rejected by men; a man of sorrows, and acquainted with grief; and as one from whom men hide their faces he was despised, and we esteemed him not. *(Long pause)*

[4] Surely he has borne our griefs and carried our sorrows; yet we esteemed him stricken, smitten by God, and afflicted. [5] But he was wounded for our transgressions, he was bruised for our iniquities; upon him was the chastisement that made us whole, and with his stripes we are healed. *(Long pause)*

[6] All we like sheep have gone astray; we have turned every one to his own way; and the LORD has laid on him the iniquity of us all. *(Long pause)*

[7] He was oppressed, and he was afflicted, yet he opened not his mouth; like a lamb that is led to the slaughter, and like a sheep that before its shearers is dumb, so he opened not his mouth. *(Long pause)*

[8] By oppression and judgment he was taken away; and as for his generation, who considered that he was cut off out of the land of the living, stricken for the transgression of my people? [9] And they made his grave with the wicked and with a rich man in his death, although he had done no violence, and there was no deceit in his mouth. *(Long pause)*

[10] Yet it was the will of the LORD to bruise him; he has put him to grief; when he makes himself an offering for sin, he shall see his offspring, he shall prolong his days; the will of the LORD shall prosper in his hand; *(Long pause)*

[11] he shall see the fruit of the travail of his soul and be satisfied; by his knowledge shall the righteous one, my servant, make many to be accounted righteous; and he shall bear their iniquities. *(Long pause)*

[12] Therefore I will divide him a portion with the great, and he shall divide the spoil with the strong; because he poured out his soul to death, and was numbered with the transgressors; yet he bore the sin of many, and made intercession for the transgressors. *(Long pause)*

At the end of 15 minutes, say:

Leader: To continue, please turn to "Prayer" on page 28 in your book.

April (A)

Communal Scripture Meditation as Lectio Divina

If the First Saturday in April is during Lent, then use this meditation. Otherwise, use April (B).

Leader: To harmonize with the liturgical season of Lent, we will now meditate on the 3rd Sorrowful Mystery, the Crowning of Jesus with Thorns, beginning with Mt. 27:27.

(Pause)

Reading

Leader: O Blessed Mother, what does this Scripture say? *(basado en Verbum Domini, Pope Benedict XVI)*

^{27} Then the soldiers of the governor took Jesus into the praetorium, and they gathered the whole battalion before him. ^{28} And they stripped him and put a scarlet robe upon him, ^{29} and plaiting a crown of thorns they put it on his head, and put a reed in his right hand. And kneeling before him they mocked him, saying, "Hail, King of the Jews!"

(Pause)

Meditation

Leader: O Blessed Mother, what does this Scripture say to us, personally? *(based on Verbum Domini)*

(Long pause) (a long pause equals approximately 20 seconds)

Reading

Leader: O Blessed Mother, what does this Scripture say?

^{30} And they spat upon him, and took the reed and struck him on the head. ^{31} And when they had mocked him, they stripped him of the robe, and put his own clothes on him, and led him away to crucify him.

(Pause)

Meditation

Leader: O Blessed Mother, what does this Scripture say to us, personally?

(Long pause)

Leader: We will now meditate on the 4^h Sorrowful Mystery, Jesus Carries the Cross, beginning with Lk. 23:26.

(Pause)

Reading

Leader: O Blessed Mother, what does this Scripture say?

²⁶ And as they led him away, they seized one Simon of Cyre′ne, who was coming in from the country, and laid on him the cross, to carry it behind Jesus.

(Pause)

Meditation

Leader: O Blessed Mother, what does this Scripture say to us, personally?

(Long pause)

Reading and Meditation

The leader will continue reading Scripture verses and pausing, without asking questions. The faithful may continue to ask themselves the two questions silently after each Scripture reading.

²⁷ And there followed him a great multitude of the people, and of women who bewailed and lamented him. *(Long pause)*

After each reading, silently ask:
O Blessed Mother, what does this Scripture say?
O Blessed Mother, what does this Scripture say to me, personally?

²⁸ But Jesus turning to them said, "Daughters of Jerusalem, do not weep for me, but weep for yourselves and for your children. *(Long pause)*

²⁹ For behold, the days are coming when they will say, 'Blessed are the barren, and the wombs that never bore, and the breasts that never gave suck!' *(Long pause)*

³⁰ Then they will begin to say to the mountains, 'Fall on us'; and to the hills, 'Cover us.' ³¹ For if they do this when the wood is green, what will happen when it is dry?" *(Long pause)*

Leader: We will now meditate on the 5th Sorrowful Mystery, the Crucifixion and Death of Our Lord, beginning with Jn. 19:17.

(Pause)

17 So they took Jesus, and he went out, bearing his own cross, to the place called the place of a skull, which is called in Hebrew Gol'gotha. 18 There they crucified him, and with him two others, one on either side, and Jesus between them. *(Long pause)*

19 Pilate also wrote a title and put it on the cross; it read, "Jesus of Nazareth, the King of the Jews." 20 Many of the Jews read this title, for the place where Jesus was crucified was near the city; and it was written in Hebrew, in Latin, and in Greek. *(Long pause)*

21 The chief priests of the Jews then said to Pilate, "Do not write, 'The King of the Jews,' but, 'This man said, I am King of the Jews.'" 22 Pilate answered, "What I have written I have written." *(Long pause)*

23 When the soldiers had crucified Jesus they took his garments and made four parts, one for each soldier; also his tunic. But the tunic was without seam, woven from top to bottom; 24 so they said to one another, "Let us not tear it, but cast lots for it to see whose it shall be." *(Long pause)*

This was to fulfil the scripture, "They parted my garments among them, and for my clothing they cast lots." 25 So the soldiers did this. *(Long pause)*

But standing by the cross of Jesus were his mother, and his mother's sister, Mary the wife of Clopas, and Mary Mag'dalene. 26 When Jesus saw his mother, and the disciple whom he loved standing near, he said to his mother, "Woman, behold, your son!" *(Long pause)*

27 Then he said to the disciple, "Behold, your mother!" And from that hour the disciple took her to his own home. *(Long pause)*

28 After this Jesus, knowing that all was now finished, said (to fulfil the Scripture), "I thirst." 29 A bowl full of vinegar stood there; so they put a sponge full of the vinegar on hyssop and held it to his mouth. 30 When Jesus had received

the vinegar, he said, "It is finished"; and he bowed his head and gave up his spirit. *(Long pause)*

[31] Since it was the day of Preparation, in order to prevent the bodies from remaining on the cross on the sabbath (for that sabbath was a high day), the Jews asked Pilate that their legs might be broken, and that they might be taken away. *(Long pause)*

[32] So the soldiers came and broke the legs of the first, and of the other who had been crucified with him; [33] but when they came to Jesus and saw that he was already dead, they did not break his legs. *(Long pause)*

[34] But one of the soldiers pierced his side with a spear, and at once there came out blood and water. [35] He who saw it has borne witness—his testimony is true, and he knows that he tells the truth—that you also may believe. *(Long pause)*

[36] For these things took place that the scripture might be fulfilled, "Not a bone of him shall be broken." [37] And again another scripture says, "They shall look on him whom they have pierced." *(Long pause)*

At the end of 15 minutes, say:

Leader: To continue, please turn to "Prayer" on page 28 in your book.

April (B)

Communal Scripture Meditation as Lectio Divina

If the First Saturday in April is during the Easter Season, then use this meditation. Otherwise, use April (A).

Leader: To harmonize with the liturgical season of Easter, we will now meditate on the 1st Glorious Mystery, the Resurrection of Jesus from the Dead beginning with Jn. 20:11.

(Pause)

Reading

Leader: O Blessed Mother, what does this Scripture say? *(basado en Verbum Domini, Pope Benedict XVI)*

[11] But Mary stood weeping outside the tomb, and as she wept she stooped to look into the tomb; [12] and she saw two angels in white, sitting where the body of Jesus had lain, one at the head and one at the feet.

(Pause)

Meditation

Leader: O Blessed Mother, what does this Scripture say to us, personally? *(based on Verbum Domini)*

(Long pause) (a long pause equals approximately 20 seconds)

Reading

Leader: O Blessed Mother, what does this Scripture say?

[13] They said to her, "Woman, why are you weeping?" She said to them, "Because they have taken away my Lord, and I do not know where they have laid him." [14] Saying this, she turned round and saw Jesus standing, but she did not know that it was Jesus.

(Pause)

Meditation

Leader: O Blessed Mother, what does this Scripture say to us, personally?

(Long pause)

Reading and Meditation

The leader will continue reading Scripture verses and pausing, without asking questions, until the next mystery. The faithful may continue to ask themselves the two questions silently after each Scripture reading.

[15] Jesus said to her, "Woman, why are you weeping? Whom do you seek?" Supposing him to be [15] Jesus said to her, "Woman why are you weeping? Whom do you seek?" Supposing him to be the gardener, she said to him, "Sir, if you have carried him away, tell me where you have laid him, and I will take him away." *(Long pause)*

After each reading, silently ask:
O Blessed Mother, what does this Scripture say?
O Blessed Mother, what does this Scripture say to me, personally?

[16] Jesus said to her, "Mary." She turned and said to him in Hebrew, "Rab-bo′ni!" (which means Teacher). [17] Jesus said to her, "Do not hold me, for I have not yet ascended to the Father; but go to my brethren and say to them, I am ascending to my Father and your Father, to my God and your God." [18] Mary Mag′dalene went and said to the disciples, "I have seen the Lord"; and she told them that he had said these things to her. *(Long pause)*

[19] On the evening of that day, the first day of the week, the doors being shut where the disciples were, for fear of the Jews, Jesus came and stood among them and said to them, "Peace be with you." *(Long pause)*

[20] When he had said this, he showed them his hands and his side. Then the disciples were glad when they saw the Lord. [21] Jesus said to them again, "Peace be with you. As the Father has sent me, even so I send you." *(Long pause)*

[22] And when he had said this, he breathed on them, and said to them, "Receive the Holy Spirit. [23] If you forgive the sins of any, they are forgiven; if you retain the sins of any, they are retained." *(Long pause)*

[24] Now Thomas, one of the twelve, called the Twin, was not with them when Jesus came. [25] So the other disciples told him, "We have seen the Lord." But he said to them, "Unless I see in his hands the print of the nails, and place my finger in the mark of the nails, and place my hand in his side, I will not believe." *(Long pause)*

[26] Eight days later, his disciples were again in the house, and Thomas was with them. The doors were shut, but Jesus came and stood among them, and said, "Peace be with you." [27] Then he said to Thomas, "Put your finger here, and see my hands; and put out your hand, and place it in my side; do not be faithless, but believing." *(Long pause)*

[28] Thomas answered him, "My Lord and my God!" [29] Jesus said to him, "Have you believed because you have seen me? Blessed are those who have not seen and yet believe." *(Long pause)*

Leader: We will now meditate on the 2nd Glorious Mystery, the Ascension of Jesus into Heaven, beginning with Acts 1,6.

(Pause)

Reading

Leader: O Blessed Mother, what does this Scripture say?

[6] So when they had come together, they asked him, "Lord, will you at this time restore the kingdom to Israel?" [7] He said to them, "It is not for you to know times or seasons which the Father has fixed by his own authority.

(Pause)

Meditation

Leader: O Blessed Mother, what does this Scripture say to us, personally?

(Long pause)

Reading and Meditation

The leader will continue reading Scripture verses and pausing, without asking questions. The faithful may continue to ask themselves the two questions silently after each Scripture reading.

[8] But you shall receive power when the Holy Spirit has come upon you; and you shall be my witnesses in Jerusalem and in all Judea and Samar'ia and to the end of the earth." [9] And when he had said this, as they were looking on, he was lifted up, and a cloud took him out of their sight. *(Long pause)*

[10] And while they were gazing into heaven as he went, behold, two men stood by them in white robes, [11] and said, "Men of Galilee, why do you stand looking into

heaven? This Jesus, who was taken up from you into heaven, will come in the same way as you saw him go into heaven." *(Long pause)*

[12] Then they returned to Jerusalem from the mount called Olivet, which is near Jerusalem, a sabbath day's journey away; [13] and when they had entered, they went up to the upper room, where they were staying, Peter and John and James and Andrew, Philip and Thomas, Bartholomew and Matthew, James the son of Alphaeus and Simon the Zealot and Judas the son of James. *(Long pause)*

[14] All these with one accord devoted themselves to prayer, together with the women and Mary the mother of Jesus, and with his brethren. *(Long pause)*

Leader: We will now meditate on the 3rd Glorious Mystery, the Descent of the Holy Spirit upon Mary and the Apostles, beginning with Acts 2:1.

(Pause)

2 When the day of Pentecost had come, they were all together in one place. [2] And suddenly a sound came from heaven like the rush of a mighty wind, and it filled all the house where they were sitting. *(Long pause)*

[3] And there appeared to them tongues as of fire, distributed and resting on each one of them. [4] And they were all filled with the Holy Spirit and began to speak in other tongues, as the Spirit gave them utterance. *(Long pause)*

[5] Now there were dwelling in Jerusalem Jews, devout men from every nation under heaven. [6] And at this sound the multitude came together, and they were bewildered, because each one heard them speaking in his own language. *(Long pause)*

[7] And they were amazed and wondered, saying, "Are not all these who are speaking Galileans? [8] And how is it that we hear, each of us in his own native language? *(Long pause)*

[9] Par'thians and Medes and E'lamites and residents of Mesopota'mia, Judea and Cappado'cia, Pontus and Asia, [10] Phryg'ia and Pamphyl'ia, Egypt and the parts of Libya belonging to Cyre'ne, and visitors from Rome, both Jews and proselytes, [11] Cretans and Arabians, we hear them telling in our own tongues the mighty works of God." *(Long pause)*

At the end of 15 minutes, say:

Leader: To continue, please turn to "Prayer" on page 28 in your book.

May (A)

Communal Scripture Meditation as Lectio Divina

If the First Saturday in April was during Lent, then use this meditation. Otherwise, use May (B).

Leader: To harmonize with the liturgical season of Easter, we will now meditate on the 1st Glorious Mystery, the Resurrection of Jesus from the Dead, beginning with Jn. 20:11.

(Pause)

Reading

Leader: O Blessed Mother, what does this Scripture say? *(basado en Verbum Domini, Pope Benedict XVI)*

[11] But Mary stood weeping outside the tomb, and as she wept she stooped to look into the tomb; [12] and she saw two angels in white, sitting where the body of Jesus had lain, one at the head and one at the feet.

(Pause)

Meditation

Leader: O Blessed Mother, what does this Scripture say to us, personally? *(based on Verbum Domini)*

(Long pause) (a long pause equals approximately 20 seconds)

Reading

Leader: O Blessed Mother, what does this Scripture say?

[13] They said to her, "Woman, why are you weeping?" She said to them, "Because they have taken away my Lord, and I do not know where they have laid him." [14] Saying this, she turned round and saw Jesus standing, but she did not know that it was Jesus.

(Pause)

Meditation

Leader: O Blessed Mother, what does this Scripture say to us, personally?

(Long pause)

Reading and Meditation

The leader will continue reading Scripture verses and pausing, without asking questions, until the next mystery. The faithful may continue to ask themselves the two questions silently after each Scripture reading.

[15] Jesus said to her, "Woman, why are you weeping? Whom do you seek?" Supposing him to be the gardener, she said to him, "Sir, if you have carried him away, tell me where you have laid him, and I will take him away." *(Long pause)*

After each reading, silently ask:
O Blessed Mother, what does this Scripture say?
O Blessed Mother, what does this Scripture say to me, personally?

[16] Jesus said to her, "Mary." She turned and said to him in Hebrew, "Rab-bo'ni!" (which means Teacher). [17] Jesus said to her, "Do not hold me, for I have not yet ascended to the Father; but go to my brethren and say to them, I am ascending to my Father and your Father, to my God and your God." [18] Mary Mag'dalene went and said to the disciples, "I have seen the Lord"; and she told them that he had said these things to her. *(Long pause)*

[19] On the evening of that day, the first day of the week, the doors being shut where the disciples were, for fear of the Jews, Jesus came and stood among them and said to them, "Peace be with you." *(Long pause)*

[20] When he had said this, he showed them his hands and his side. Then the disciples were glad when they saw the Lord. [21] Jesus said to them again, "Peace be with you. As the Father has sent me, even so I send you." *(Long pause)*

[22] And when he had said this, he breathed on them, and said to them, "Receive the Holy Spirit. [23] If you forgive the sins of any, they are forgiven; if you retain the sins of any, they are retained." *(Long pause)*

[24] Now Thomas, one of the twelve, called the Twin, was not with them when Jesus came. [25] So the other disciples told him, "We have seen the Lord." But he said to them, "Unless I see in his hands the print of the nails, and place my finger in the mark of the nails, and place my hand in his side, I will not believe." *(Long pause)*

[26] Eight days later, his disciples were again in the house, and Thomas was with them. The doors were shut, but Jesus came and stood among them, and said, "Peace be with you." [27] Then he said to Thomas, "Put your finger here, and see my hands; and put out your hand, and place it in my side; do not be faithless, but believing." *(Long pause)*

[28] Thomas answered him, "My Lord and my God!" [29] Jesus said to him, "Have you believed because you have seen me? Blessed are those who have not seen and yet believe." *(Long pause)*

Leader: We will now meditate on the 2nd Glorious Mystery, the Ascension of Jesus into Heaven, beginning with Acts 1:6.

(Pause)

Reading

Leader: O Blessed Mother, what does this Scripture say?

[6] So when they had come together, they asked him, "Lord, will you at this time restore the kingdom to Israel?" [7] He said to them, "It is not for you to know times or seasons which the Father has fixed by his own authority.

(Pause)

Meditation

Leader: O Blessed Mother, what does this Scripture say to us, personally?

(Long pause)

Reading and Meditation

The leader will continue reading Scripture verses and pausing, without asking questions. The faithful may continue to ask themselves the two questions silently after each Scripture reading.

[8] But you shall receive power when the Holy Spirit has come upon you; and you shall be my witnesses in Jerusalem and in all Judea and Samar'ia and to the end of the earth." [9] And when he had said this, as they were looking on, he was lifted up, and a cloud took him out of their sight. *(Long pause)*

[10] And while they were gazing into heaven as he went, behold, two men stood by them in white robes, [11] and said, "Men of Galilee, why do you stand looking into heaven? This Jesus, who was taken up from you into heaven, will come in the same way as you saw him go into heaven." *(Long pause)*

[12] Then they returned to Jerusalem from the mount called Olivet, which is near Jerusalem, a sabbath day's journey away; [13] and when they had entered, they went up to the upper room, where they were staying, Peter and John and James and Andrew, Philip and Thomas, Bartholomew and Matthew, James the son of Alphaeus and Simon the Zealot and Judas the son of James. *(Long pause)*

[14] All these with one accord devoted themselves to prayer, together with the women and Mary the mother of Jesus, and with his brethren. *(Long pause)*

Leader: We will now meditate on the 3rd Glorious Mystery, the Descent of the Holy Spirit upon Mary and the Apostles, beginning with Acts 2:1.

(Pause)

2 When the day of Pentecost had come, they were all together in one place. [2] And suddenly a sound came from heaven like the rush of a mighty wind, and it filled all the house where they were sitting. *(Long pause)*

³ And there appeared to them tongues as of fire, distributed and resting on each one of them. ⁴ And they were all filled with the Holy Spirit and began to speak in other tongues, as the Spirit gave them utterance. *(Long pause)*

⁵ Now there were dwelling in Jerusalem Jews, devout men from every nation under heaven. ⁶ And at this sound the multitude came together, and they were bewildered, because each one heard them speaking in his own language. *(Long pause)*

⁷ And they were amazed and wondered, saying, "Are not all these who are speaking Galileans? ⁸ And how is it that we hear, each of us in his own native language? *(Long pause)*

⁹ Par'thians and Medes and E'lamites and residents of Mesopota'mia, Judea and Cappado'cia, Pontus and Asia, ¹⁰ Phryg'ia and Pamphyl'ia, Egypt and the parts of Libya belonging to Cyre'ne, and visitors from Rome, both Jews and proselytes, ¹¹ Cretans and Arabians, we hear them telling in our own tongues the mighty works of God." *(Long pause)*

At the end of 15 minutes, say:

Leader: To continue, please turn to "Prayer" on page 28 in your book.

May (B)

Communal Scripture Meditation as Lectio Divina

If the First Saturday in April was during the Easter Season, then use this meditation. Otherwise, use May (A).

Leader: To harmonize with the liturgical season of Easter, we will now meditate on the 2ⁿᵈ Glorious Mystery, the Ascension of Jesus into Heaven, beginning with Acts 1:6.

(Pause)

Reading

Leader: O Blessed Mother, what does this Scripture say? *(basado en Verbum Domini, Pope Benedict XVI)*

[6] So when they had come together, they asked him, "Lord, will you at this time restore the kingdom to Israel?" [7] He said to them, "It is not for you to know times or seasons which the Father has fixed by his own authority.

(Pause)

Meditation

Leader: O Blessed Mother, what does this Scripture say to us, personally? *(based on Verbum Domini)*

(Long pause) (a long pause equals approximately 20 seconds)

Reading

Leader: O Blessed Mother, what does this Scripture say?

[8] But you shall receive power when the Holy Spirit has come upon you; and you shall be my witnesses in Jerusalem and in all Judea and Samar′ia and to the end of the earth." [9] And when he had said this, as they were looking on, he was lifted up, and a cloud took him out of their sight.

(Pause)

Meditation

Leader: O Blessed Mother, what does this Scripture say to us, personally?

(Long pause)

Reading and Meditation

The leader will continue reading Scripture verses and pausing, without asking questions, until the next mystery. The faithful may continue to ask themselves the two questions silently after each Scripture reading.

¹⁰ And while they were gazing into heaven as he went, behold, two men stood by them in white robes, ¹¹ and said, "Men of Galilee, why do you stand looking into heaven? This Jesus, who was taken up from you into heaven, will come in the same way as you saw him go into heaven." *(Long pause)*

After each reading, silently ask:
O Blessed Mother, what does this Scripture say?
O Blessed Mother, what does this Scripture say to me, personally?

¹² Then they returned to Jerusalem from the mount called Olivet, which is near Jerusalem, a sabbath day's journey away; ¹³ and when they had entered, they went up to the upper room, where they were staying, Peter and John and James and Andrew, Philip and Thomas, Bartholomew and Matthew, James the son of Alphaeus and Simon the Zealot and Judas the son of James. *(Long pause)*

¹⁴ All these with one accord devoted themselves to prayer, together with the women and Mary the mother of Jesus, and with his brethren. *(Long pause)*

Leader: We will now meditate on the 3ʳᵈ Glorious Mystery, the Descent of the Holy Spirit upon Mary and the Apostles, beginning with Acts 2:1.

(Pause)

Reading

Leader: O Blessed Mother, what does this Scripture say?

2 When the day of Pentecost had come, they were all together in one place. ² And suddenly a sound came from heaven like the rush of a mighty wind, and it filled all the house where they were sitting.

(Pause)

Meditation

Leader: O Blessed Mother, what does this Scripture say to us, personally?

(Long pause)

Reading and Meditation

65

The leader will continue reading Scripture verses and pausing, without asking questions. The faithful may continue to ask themselves the two questions silently after each Scripture reading.

³ And there appeared to them tongues as of fire, distributed and resting on each one of them. ⁴ And they were all filled with the Holy Spirit and began to speak in other tongues, as the Spirit gave them utterance. *(Long pause)*

⁵ Now there were dwelling in Jerusalem Jews, devout men from every nation under heaven. ⁶ And at this sound the multitude came together, and they were bewildered, because each one heard them speaking in his own language. *(Long pause)*

⁷ And they were amazed and wondered, saying, "Are not all these who are speaking Galileans? ⁸ And how is it that we hear, each of us in his own native language? *(Long pause)*

⁹ Par'thians and Medes and E'lamites and residents of Mesopota'mia, Judea and Cappado'cia, Pontus and Asia, ¹⁰ Phryg'ia and Pamphyl'ia, Egypt and the parts of Libya belonging to Cyre'ne, and visitors from Rome, both Jews and proselytes, ¹¹ Cretans and Arabians, we hear them telling in our own tongues the mighty works of God." *(Long pause)*

Leader: Since it is the month of May in which we honor Our Blessed Mother in a special way, we will now meditate on the 5ᵗʰ Glorious Mystery, the Crowning of Mary as Queen of Heaven and Earth, beginning with Est. 10:1.

(Pause)

10 King Ahasu-e'rus laid tribute on the land and on the coastlands of the sea. ² And all the acts of his power and might, and the full account of the high honor of Mor'decai, to which the king advanced him, are they not written in the Book of the Chronicles of the kings of Media and Persia? ³ For Mor'decai the Jew was next in rank to King Ahasu-e'rus, and he was great among the Jews and popular with the multitude of his brethren, for he sought the welfare of his people and spoke peace to all his people. *(Long pause)*

⁴ And Mor'decai said, "These things have come from God. ⁵ For I remember the dream that I had concerning these matters, and none of them has failed to be

fulfilled. [6] The tiny spring which became a river, and there was light and the sun and abundant water—the river is Esther, whom the king married and made queen. *(Long pause)*

[7] The two dragons are Haman and myself. [8] The nations are those that gathered to destroy the name of the Jews. [9] And my nation, this is Israel, who cried out to God and were saved. The Lord has saved his people; the Lord has delivered us from all these evils; God has done great signs and wonders, which have not occurred among the nations. *(Long pause)*

Leader: We now continue with passages from Wis. 7.

[8] I preferred her to scepters and thrones, and I accounted wealth as nothing in comparison with her. [9] Neither did I liken to her any priceless gem, because all gold is but a little sand in her sight, and silver will be accounted as clay before her. *(Long pause)*

[10] I loved her more than health and beauty, and I chose to have her rather than light, because her radiance never ceases. [11] All good things came to me along with her, and in her hands uncounted wealth. *(Long pause)*

[12] I rejoiced in them all, because wisdom leads them; but I did not know that she was their mother. *(Long pause)*

[13] I learned without guile and I impart without grudging; I do not hide her wealth, [14] for it is an unfailing treasure for men; those who get it obtain friendship with God, commended for the gifts that come from instruction. *(Long pause)*

Leader: We now continue with passages from Rev. 12.

12 And a great portent appeared in heaven, a woman clothed with the sun, with the moon under her feet, and on her head a crown of twelve stars; [2] she was with child and she cried out in her pangs of birth, in anguish for delivery. *(Long pause)*

[3] And another portent appeared in heaven; behold, a great red dragon, with seven heads and ten horns, and seven diadems upon his heads. [4] His tail swept down a third of the stars of heaven, and cast them to the earth. *(Long pause)*

67

And the dragon stood before the woman who was about to bear a child, that he might devour her child when she brought it forth; ⁵ she brought forth a male child, one who is to rule all the nations with a rod of iron, but her child was caught up to God and to his throne, *(Long pause)*

⁶ and the woman fled into the wilderness, where she has a place prepared by God, in which to be nourished for one thousand two hundred and sixty days. *(Long pause)*

> *At the end of 15 minutes, say:*

Leader: To continue, please turn to "Prayer" on page 28 in your book.

June

Communal Scripture Meditation as Lectio Divina

Leader: Calling to mind the liturgical solemnity of The Most Holy Body and Blood of Christ, we will now meditate on the 5ᵗʰ Luminous Mystery, the Institution of the Holy Eucharist, beginning with Jn. 6:30.

> *(Pause)*

Reading

Leader: O Blessed Mother, what does this Scripture say? *(basado en Verbum Domini, Pope Benedict XVI)*

30 So they said to him, "What sign can you do, that we may see and believe in you? What can you do?
31 Our ancestors ate manna in the desert, as it is written:
'He gave them bread from heaven to eat.'"

> *(Pause)*

Meditation

Leader: O Blessed Mother, what does this Scripture say to us, personally? *(based on Verbum Domini)*

(Long pause) (a long pause equals approximately 20 seconds)

Reading

Leader: O Blessed Mother, what does this Scripture say?

32 So Jesus said to them, "Amen, amen, I say to you, it was not Moses who gave the bread from heaven; my Father gives you the true bread from heaven.
33 For the bread of God is that which comes down from heaven and gives life to the world."

(Pause)

Meditation

Leader: O Blessed Mother, what does this Scripture say to us, personally?

(Long pause)

Reading and Meditation

The leader will continue reading Scripture verses and pausing, without asking questions, until the next mystery. The faithful may continue to ask themselves the two questions silently after each Scripture reading.

34 So they said to him, "Sir, give us this bread always."
35 Jesus said to them, "I am the bread of life; whoever comes to me will never hunger, and whoever believes in me will never thirst. *(Long pause)*

After each reading, silently ask:
O Blessed Mother, what does this Scripture say?
O Blessed Mother, what does this Scripture say to me, personally?

36 But I told you that although you have seen [me], you do not believe.
37 Everything that the Father gives me will come to me, and I will not reject anyone who comes to me,
38 because I came down from heaven not to do my own will but the will of the one who sent me. *(Long pause)*

39 And this is the will of the one who sent me, that I should not lose anything of what he gave me, but that I should raise it [on] the last day.
40 For this is the will of my Father, that everyone who sees the Son and believes in him may have eternal life, and I shall raise him [on] the last day." *(Long pause)*

52 The Jews quarreled among themselves, saying, "How can this man give us [his] flesh to eat?" 53 Jesus said to them, "Amen, amen, I say to you, unless you eat the flesh of the Son of Man and drink his blood, you do not have life within you. *(Long pause)*

54 Whoever eats my flesh and drinks my blood has eternal life, and I will raise him on the last day.
55 For my flesh is true food, and my blood is true drink.
56 Whoever eats my flesh and drinks my blood remains in me and I in him. *(Long pause)*

57 Just as the living Father sent me and I have life because of the Father, so also the one who feeds on me will have life because of me. *(Long pause)*

58 This is the bread that came down from heaven. Unlike your ancestors who ate and still died, whoever eats this bread will live forever."
59 These things he said while teaching in the synagogue in Capernaum. *(Long pause)*

Leader: We now continue with passages from 1 Cor. 11.

27 Therefore whoever eats the bread or drinks the cup of the Lord unworthily will have to answer for the body and blood of the Lord. *(Long pause)*

28 A person should examine himself, and so eat the bread and drink the cup.
29 For anyone who eats and drinks without discerning the body, eats and drinks judgment on himself. *(Long pause)*

30 That is why many among you are ill and infirm, and a considerable number are dying. *(Long pause)*

31 If we discerned ourselves, we would not be under judgment;
32 but since we are judged by [the] Lord, we are being disciplined so that we may not be condemned along with the world. *(Long pause)*

Leader: We will now meditate on the 3rd Glorious Mystery, the Descent of the Holy Spirit upon Mary and the Apostles, beginning with Acts 2:1.

(Pause)

Reading

Leader: O Blessed Mother, what does this Scripture say?

2 When the day of Pentecost had come, they were all together in one place. ² And suddenly a sound came from heaven like the rush of a mighty wind, and it filled all the house where they were sitting.

(Pause)

Meditation

Leader: O Blessed Mother, what does this Scripture say to us, personally?

(Long pause)

Reading and Meditation

The leader will continue reading Scripture verses and pausing, without asking questions. The faithful may continue to ask themselves the two questions silently after each Scripture reading.

³ And there appeared to them tongues as of fire, distributed and resting on each one of them. ⁴ And they were all filled with the Holy Spirit and began to speak in other tongues, as the Spirit gave them utterance. *(Long pause)*

⁵ Now there were dwelling in Jerusalem Jews, devout men from every nation under heaven. ⁶ And at this sound the multitude came together, and they were bewildered, because each one heard them speaking in his own language. *(Long pause)*

⁷ And they were amazed and wondered, saying, "Are not all these who are speaking Galileans? ⁸ And how is it that we hear, each of us in his own native language? *(Long pause)*

71

⁹ Par'thians and Medes and E'lamites and residents of Mesopota'mia, Judea and Cappado'cia, Pontus and Asia, ¹⁰ Phryg'ia and Pamphyl'ia, Egypt and the parts of Libya belonging to Cyre'ne, and visitors from Rome, both Jews and proselytes ¹¹ Cretans and Arabians, we hear them telling in our own tongues the mighty works of God." *(Long pause)*

At the end of 15 minutes, say:

Leader: To continue, please turn to "Prayer" on page 28 in your book.

July

Communal Scripture Meditation as Lectio Divina

Leader: We will now meditate on the 2ⁿᵈ Luminous Mystery, the Marriage Feast at Cana, beginning with Jn. 2:1.

(Pause)

Reading

Leader: O Blessed Mother, what does this Scripture say? *(basado en Verbum Domini, Pope Benedict XVI)*

1 On the third day there was a wedding in Cana in Galilee, and the mother of Jesus was there.
2 Jesus and his disciples were also invited to the wedding.

(Pause)

Meditation

Leader: O Blessed Mother, what does this Scripture say to us, personally? *(based on Verbum Domini)*

(Long pause) (a long pause equals approximately 20 seconds)

Reading

Leader: O Blessed Mother, what does this Scripture say?

3 When the wine ran short, the mother of Jesus said to him, "They have no wine."
4 [And] Jesus said to her, "Woman, how does your concern affect me? My hour has not yet come."

(Pause)

Meditation

Leader: O Blessed Mother, what does this Scripture say to us, personally?

(Long pause)

Reading and Meditation

The leader will continue reading Scripture verses and pausing, without asking questions, until the next mystery. The faithful may continue to ask themselves the two questions silently after each Scripture reading.

5 His mother said to the servers, "Do whatever he tells you." *(Long pause)*

After each reading, silently ask:
O Blessed Mother, what does this Scripture say?
O Blessed Mother, what does this Scripture say to me, personally?

6 Now there were six stone water jars there for Jewish ceremonial washings, each holding twenty to thirty gallons.
7 Jesus told them, "Fill the jars with water." So they filled them to the brim. *(Long pause)*

8 Then he told them, "Draw some out now and take it to the headwaiter." So they took it.
9 And when the headwaiter tasted the water that had become wine, without knowing where it came from (although the servers who had drawn the water knew), the headwaiter called the bridegroom *(Long pause)*

10 and said to him, "Everyone serves good wine first, and then when people have drunk freely, an inferior one; but you have kept the good wine until now." *(Long pause)*

11 Jesus did this as the beginning of his signs in Cana in Galilee and so revealed his glory, and his disciples began to believe in him.
12 After this, he and his mother, [his] brothers, and his disciples went down to Capernaum and stayed there only a few days. *(Long pause)*

Leader: We will now meditate on the 5th Glorious Mystery, the Crowning of Mary as Queen of Heaven and Earth, beginning with Est. 10:1.

(Pause)

Reading

Leader: O Blessed Mother, what does this Scripture say?

10 King Ahasu-e′rus laid tribute on the land and on the coastlands of the sea. ² And all the acts of his power and might, and the full account of the high honor of Mor′decai, to which the king advanced him, are they not written in the Book of the Chronicles of the kings of Media and Persia? ³ For Mor′decai the Jew was next in rank to King Ahasu-e′rus, and he was great among the Jews and popular with the multitude of his brethren, for he sought the welfare of his people and spoke peace to all his people.

(Pause)

Meditation

Leader: O Blessed Mother, what does this Scripture say to us, personally?

(Long pause)

Reading and Meditation

The leader will continue reading Scripture verses and pausing, without asking questions. The faithful may continue to ask themselves the two questions silently after each Scripture reading.

[4] And Mor'decai said, "These things have come from God. [5] For I remember the dream that I had concerning these matters, and none of them has failed to be fulfilled. [6] The tiny spring which became a river, and there was light and the sun and abundant water—the river is Esther, whom the king married and made queen. *(Long pause)*

[7] The two dragons are Haman and myself. [8] The nations are those that gathered to destroy the name of the Jews. [9] And my nation, this is Israel, who cried out to God and were saved. The Lord has saved his people; the Lord has delivered us from all these evils; God has done great signs and wonders, which have not occurred among the nations. *(Long pause)*

Leader: We now continue with passages from Wis. 7.

[8] I preferred her to scepters and thrones, and I accounted wealth as nothing in comparison with her. [9] Neither did I liken to her any priceless gem, because all gold is but a little sand in her sight, and silver will be accounted as clay before her. *(Long pause)*

[10] I loved her more than health and beauty, and I chose to have her rather than light, because her radiance never ceases. [11] All good things came to me along with her, and in her hands uncounted wealth. *(Long pause)*

[12] I rejoiced in them all, because wisdom leads them; but I did not know that she was their mother. *(Long pause)*

[13] I learned without guile and I impart without grudging; I do not hide her wealth, [14] for it is an unfailing treasure for men; those who get it obtain friendship with God, commended for the gifts that come from instruction. *(Long pause)*

Leader: We now continue with passages from Rev. 12.

12 And a great portent appeared in heaven, a woman clothed with the sun, with the moon under her feet, and on her head a crown of twelve stars; [2] she was with child and she cried out in her pangs of birth, in anguish for delivery. *(Long pause)*

[3] And another portent appeared in heaven; behold, a great red dragon, with seven heads and ten horns, and seven diadems upon his heads. [4] His tail swept down a third of the stars of heaven, and cast them to the earth. *(Long pause)*

And the dragon stood before the woman who was about to bear a child, that he might devour her child when she brought it forth; ⁵ she brought forth a male child, one who is to rule all the nations with a rod of iron, but her child was caught up to God and to his throne, *(Long pause)*

⁶ and the woman fled into the wilderness, where she has a place prepared by God, in which to be nourished for one thousand two hundred and sixty days. *(Long pause)*

At the end of 15 minutes, say:

Leader: To continue, please turn to "Prayer" on page 28 in your book.

August

Communal Scripture Meditation as Lectio Divina

Leader: In harmony with the liturgical feast, we will now meditate on the 4ᵗʰ Luminous Mystery, the Transfiguration of Jesus Christ, beginning with Mt. 17:1.

(Pause)

Reading

Leader: O Blessed Mother, what does this Scripture say? *(basado en Verbum Domini, Pope Benedict XVI)*

1 After six days Jesus took Peter, James, and John his brother, and led them up a high mountain by themselves.
2 And he was transfigured before them; his face shone like the sun and his clothes became white as light.

(Pause)

Meditation

Leader: O Blessed Mother, what does this Scripture say to us, personally? *(based on Verbum Domini)*

(Long pause) (a long pause equals approximately 20 seconds)

Reading

Leader: O Blessed Mother, what does this Scripture say?

3 And behold, Moses and Elijah appeared to them, conversing with him.
4 Then Peter said to Jesus in reply, "Lord, it is good that we are here. If you wish, I will make three tents here, one for you, one for Moses, and one for Elijah."

(Pause)

Meditation

Leader: O Blessed Mother, what does this Scripture say to us, personally?

(Long pause)

Reading and Meditation

The leader will continue reading Scripture verses and pausing, without asking questions, until the next mystery. The faithful may continue to ask themselves the two questions silently after each Scripture reading.

5 While he was still speaking, behold, a bright cloud cast a shadow over them, then from the cloud came a voice that said, "This is my beloved Son, with whom I am well pleased; listen to him." *(Long pause)*

After each reading, silently ask:
O Blessed Mother, what does this Scripture say?
O Blessed Mother, what does this Scripture say to me, personally?

6 When the disciples heard this, they fell prostrate and were very much afraid.
7 But Jesus came and touched them, saying, "Rise, and do not be afraid."
8 And when the disciples raised their eyes, they saw no one else but Jesus alone.
(Long pause)

Leader: To harmonize with a liturgical solemnity we will celebrate this month we will now meditate on the 4th Glorious Mystery, the Assumption of Mary into Heaven, beginning with Rev. 11:15.

(Pause)

Reading

Leader: O Blessed Mother, what does this Scripture say?

[15] Then the seventh angel blew his trumpet, and there were loud voices in heaven saying, "The kingdom of the world has become the kingdom of our Lord and of his Christ, and he shall reign for ever and ever."

(Pause)

Meditation

Leader: O Blessed Mother, what does this Scripture say to us, personally?

(Long pause)

Reading and Meditation

The leader will continue reading Scripture verses and pausing, without asking questions. The faithful may continue to ask themselves the two questions silently after each Scripture reading.

[16] And the twenty-four elders who sit on their thrones before God fell on their faces and worshiped God, [17] saying, "We give thanks to thee, Lord God Almighty, who art and who wast, that thou hast taken thy great power and begun to reign. *(Long pause)*

[18] The nations raged, but thy wrath came, and the time for the dead to be judged for rewarding thy servants, the prophets and saints, and those who fear thy name, both small and great, and for destroying the destroyers of the earth." *(Long pause)*

[19] Then God's temple in heaven was opened, and the ark of his covenant was seen within his temple; and there were flashes of lightning, loud noises, peals of thunder, an earthquake, and heavy hail. *(Long pause)*

[1] And a great portent appeared in heaven, a woman clothed with the sun, with the moon under her feet, and on her head a crown of twelve stars; [2] she was with child and she cried out in her pangs of birth, in anguish for delivery. *(Long pause)*

[3] And another portent appeared in heaven; behold, a great red dragon, with seven heads and ten horns, and seven diadems upon his heads. [4] His tail swept down a third of the stars of heaven, and cast them to the earth. *(Long pause)*

And the dragon stood before the woman who was about to bear a child, that he might devour her child when she brought it forth; [5] she brought forth a male child, one who is to rule all the nations with a rod of iron, but her child was caught up to God and to his throne, *(Long pause)*

[6] and the woman fled into the wilderness, where she has a place prepared by God, in which to be nourished for one thousand two hundred and sixty days. *(Long pause)*

Leader: We now continue with passages from Heb. 4.

4 Therefore, while the promise of entering his rest remains, let us fear lest any of you be judged to have failed to reach it. [2] For good news came to us just as to them; but the message which they heard did not benefit them, because it did not meet with faith in the hearers. *(Long pause)*

[3] For we who have believed enter that rest, as he has said, "As I swore in my wrath, 'They shall never enter my rest,'" although his works were finished from the foundation of the world. [4] For he has somewhere spoken of the seventh day in this way, "And God rested on the seventh day from all his works." *(Long pause)*

[5] And again in this place he said, "They shall never enter my rest." *(Long pause)*

[6] Since therefore it remains for some to enter it, and those who formerly received the good news failed to enter because of disobedience, [7] again he sets a certain day, "Today," saying through David so long afterward, in the words already

quoted, "Today, when you hear his voice, do not harden your hearts." *(Long pause)*

[8] For if Joshua had given them rest, God would not speak later of another day. [9] So then, there remains a sabbath rest for the people of God; [10] for whoever enters God's rest also ceases from his labors as God did from his. [11] Let us therefore strive to enter that rest, that no one fall by the same sort of disobedience. *(Long pause)*

[12] For the Word of God is living and active, sharper than any two-edged sword, piercing to the division of soul and spirit, of joints and marrow, and discerning the thoughts and intentions of the heart. [13] And before him no creature is hidden, but all are open and laid bare to the eyes of him with whom we have to do. *(Long pause)*

[14] Since then we have a great high priest who has passed through the heavens, Jesus, the Son of God, let us hold fast our confession. [15] For we have not a high priest who is unable to sympathize with our weaknesses, but one who in every respect has been tempted as we are, yet without sinning. [16] Let us then with confidence draw near to the throne of grace, that we may receive mercy and find grace to help in time of need. *(Long pause)*

At the end of 15 minutes, say:

Leader: To continue, please turn to "Prayer" on page 28 in your book.

September

Communal Scripture Meditation as Lectio Divina

Leader: To harmonize with the liturgical celebrations of the Exaltation of the Holy Cross and Our Lady of Sorrows, we will now meditate on the 1st Sorrowful Mystery, the Agony of Jesus in the Garden, beginning with Mt. 26:36.

(Pause)

Reading

Leader: O Blessed Mother, what does this Scripture say? *(basado en Verbum Domini, Pope Benedict XVI)*

[36] Then Jesus went with them to a place called Gethsem'ane, and he said to his disciples, "Sit here, while I go yonder and pray." [37] And taking with him Peter and the two sons of Zeb'edee, he began to be sorrowful and troubled.

(Pause)

Meditation

Leader: O Blessed Mother, what does this Scripture say to us, personally? *(based on Verbum Domini)*

(Long pause) (a long pause equals approximately 20 seconds)

Reading

Leader: O Blessed Mother, what does this Scripture say?

[38] Then he said to them, "My soul is very sorrowful, even to death; remain here, and watch with me." [39] And going a little farther he fell on his face and prayed, "My Father, if it be possible, let this cup pass from me; nevertheless, not as I will, but as thou wilt."

(Pause)

Meditation

Leader: O Blessed Mother, what does this Scripture say to us, personally?

(Long pause)

Reading and Meditation

The leader will continue reading Scripture verses and pausing, without asking questions, until the next mystery. The faithful may continue to ask themselves the two questions silently after each Scripture reading.

⁴⁰ And he came to the disciples and found them sleeping; and he said to Peter, "So, could you not watch with me one hour? ⁴¹ Watch and pray that you may not enter into temptation; the spirit indeed is willing, but the flesh is weak." *(Long pause)*

After each reading, silently ask:
O Blessed Mother, what does this Scripture say?
O Blessed Mother, what does this Scripture say to me, personally?

⁴² Again, for the second time, he went away and prayed, "My Father, if this cannot pass unless I drink it, thy will be done." ⁴³ And again he came and found them sleeping, for their eyes were heavy. ⁴⁴ So, leaving them again, he went away and prayed for the third time, saying the same words. *(Long pause)*

⁴⁵ Then he came to the disciples and said to them, "Are you still sleeping and taking your rest? Behold, the hour is at hand, and the Son of man is betrayed into the hands of sinners. ⁴⁶ Rise, let us be going; see, my betrayer is at hand." *(Long pause)*

⁴⁷ While he was still speaking, Judas came, one of the twelve, and with him a great crowd with swords and clubs, from the chief priests and the elders of the people. ⁴⁸ Now the betrayer had given them a sign, saying, "The one I shall kiss is the man; seize him." *(Long pause)*

⁴⁹ And he came up to Jesus at once and said, "Hail, Master!" And he kissed him. ⁵⁰ Jesus said to him, "Friend, why are you here?" Then they came up and laid hands on Jesus and seized him. *(Long pause)*

⁵¹ And behold, one of those who were with Jesus stretched out his hand and drew his sword, and struck the slave of the high priest, and cut off his ear. ⁵² Then Jesus said to him, "Put your sword back into its place; for all who take the sword will perish by the sword. *(Long pause)*

Leader: We will now meditate on the 4ᵗʰ Sorrowful Mystery, Jesus Carries the Cross, beginning with Lk. 23: 26.

(Pause)

Reading

Leader: O Blessed Mother, what does this Scripture say?

²⁶ And as they led him away, they seized one Simon of Cyre'ne, who was coming in from the country, and laid on him the cross, to carry it behind Jesus.

(Pause)

Meditation

Leader: O Blessed Mother, what does this Scripture say to us, personally?

(Long pause)

Reading and Meditation

The leader will continue reading Scripture verses and pausing, without asking questions. The faithful may continue to ask themselves the two questions silently after each Scripture reading.

²⁷ And there followed him a great multitude of the people, and of women who bewailed and lamented him. *(Long pause)*

²⁸ But Jesus turning to them said, "Daughters of Jerusalem, do not weep for me, but weep for yourselves and for your children. *(Long pause)*

²⁹ For behold, the days are coming when they will say, 'Blessed are the barren, and the wombs that never bore, and the breasts that never gave suck!' *(Long pause)*

³⁰ Then they will begin to say to the mountains, 'Fall on us'; and to the hills, 'Cover us.' ³¹ For if they do this when the wood is green, what will happen when it is dry?" *(Long pause)*

Leader: We will now meditate on the 5ᵗʰ Sorrowful Mystery, the Crucifixion and Death of Our Lord, beginning with Jn. 19:25.

(Pause)

[25] …But standing by the cross of Jesus were his mother, and his mother's sister Mary the wife of Clopas, and Mary Mag'dalene. [26] When Jesus saw his mother and the disciple whom he loved standing near, he said to his mother, "Woman, behold, your son!" *(Long pause)*

[27] Then he said to the disciple, "Behold, your mother!" And from that hour the disciple took her to his own home. *(Long pause)*

[28] After this Jesus, knowing that all was now finished, said (to fulfil the scripture), "I thirst." [29] A bowl full of vinegar stood there; so they put a sponge full of the vinegar on hyssop and held it to his mouth. [30] When Jesus had received the vinegar, he said, "It is finished"; and he bowed his head and gave up his spirit. *(Long pause)*

[31] Since it was the day of Preparation, in order to prevent the bodies from remaining on the cross on the sabbath (for that sabbath was a high day), the Jews asked Pilate that their legs might be broken, and that they might be taken away. *(Long pause)*

[32] So the soldiers came and broke the legs of the first, and of the other who had been crucified with him; [33] but when they came to Jesus and saw that he was already dead, they did not break his legs. *(Long pause)*

[34] But one of the soldiers pierced his side with a spear, and at once there came out blood and water. [35] He who saw it has borne witness—his testimony is true, and he knows that he tells the truth—that you also may believe. *(Long pause)*

[36] For these things took place that the scripture might be fulfilled, "Not a bone of him shall be broken." [37] And again another scripture says, "They shall look on him whom they have pierced." *(Long pause)*

At the end of 15 minutes, say:

Leader: To continue, please turn to "Prayer" on page 28 in your book.

October

Communal Scripture Meditation as Lectio Divina

Leader: Recalling the need for reparation to the Immaculate Heart of Mary, we will now meditate on the 4th Joyful Mystery, the Presentation of the Child Jesus in the Temple, beginning with Lk. 2:22.

(Pause)

Reading

Leader: O Blessed Mother, what does this Scripture say? *(basado en Verbum Domini, Pope Benedict XVI*

22 When the days were completed for their purification according to the law of Moses, they took him up to Jerusalem to present him to the Lord,

(Pause)

Meditation

Leader: O Blessed Mother, what does this Scripture say to us, personally? *(based on Verbum Domini)*

(Long pause) (a long pause equals approximately 20 seconds)

Reading

Leader: O Blessed Mother, what does this Scripture say?

23 just as it is written in the law of the Lord, "Every male that opens the womb shall be consecrated to the Lord,"

(Pause)

Meditation

Leader: O Blessed Mother, what does this Scripture say to us, personally?

(Long pause)

Reading and Meditation

85

The leader will continue reading Scripture verses and pausing, without asking questions, until the next mystery. The faithful may continue to ask themselves the two questions silently after each Scripture reading.

24 and to offer the sacrifice of "a pair of turtledoves or two young pigeons," in accordance with the dictate in the law of the Lord. *(Long pause)*

After each reading, silently ask:
O Blessed Mother, what does this Scripture say?
O Blessed Mother, what does this Scripture say to me, personally?

25 Now there was a man in Jerusalem whose name was Simeon. This man was righteous and devout, awaiting the consolation of Israel, and the holy Spirit was upon him.
26 It had been revealed to him by the holy Spirit that he should not see death before he had seen the Messiah of the Lord. *(Long pause)*

27 He came in the Spirit into the temple; and when the parents brought in the child Jesus to perform the custom of the law in regard to him,
28 he took him into his arms and blessed God, saying:
29 "Now, Master, you may let your servant go in peace, according to your word, *(Long pause)*

30 for my eyes have seen your salvation,
31 which you prepared in sight of all the peoples,
32 a light for revelation to the Gentiles, and glory for your people Israel." *(Long pause)*

33 The child's father and mother were amazed at what was said about him;
34 and Simeon blessed them and said to Mary his mother, "Behold, this child is destined for the fall and rise of many in Israel, and to be a sign that will be contradicted *(Long pause)*

35 (and you yourself a sword will pierce) so that the thoughts of many hearts may be revealed." *(Long pause)*

36 There was also a prophetess, Anna, the daughter of Phanuel, of the tribe of Asher. She was advanced in years, having lived seven years with her husband after her marriage,

37 and then as a widow until she was eighty-four. She never left the temple, but worshiped night and day with fasting and prayer. *(Long pause)*

38 And coming forward at that very time, she gave thanks to God and spoke about the child to all who were awaiting the redemption of Jerusalem. *(Long pause)*

39 When they had fulfilled all the prescriptions of the law of the Lord, they returned to Galilee, to their own town of Nazareth.
40 The child grew and became strong, filled with wisdom; and the favor of God was upon him. *(Long pause)*

Leader: To encourage promoting the Gospel Prayer of the Rosary, which we celebrate this month, we will now meditate on the 3rd Luminous Mystery, the Proclamation of the Gospel, beginning with Mt. 5:1.

(Pause)

Reading

Leader: O Blessed Mother, what does this Scripture say?

1 When he saw the crowds, he went up the mountain, and after he had sat down, his disciples came to him.
2 He began to teach them, saying:
3 "Blessed are the poor in spirit,
for theirs is the kingdom of heaven.

(Pause)

Meditation

Leader: O Blessed Mother, what does this Scripture say to us, personally?

(Long pause)

Reading and Meditation

The leader will continue reading Scripture verses and pausing, without asking questions. The faithful may continue to ask themselves the two questions silently after each Scripture reading.

4 Blessed are they who mourn,
for they will be comforted.
5 Blessed are the meek,
for they will inherit the land. *(Long pause)*

6 Blessed are they who hunger and thirst for righteousness,
for they will be satisfied.
7 Blessed are the merciful,
for they will be shown mercy. *(Long pause)*

8 Blessed are the clean of heart,
for they will see God.
9 Blessed are the peacemakers,
for they will be called children of God. *(Long pause)*

10 Blessed are they who are persecuted for the sake of righteousness,
for theirs is the kingdom of heaven. *(Long pause)*

11 Blessed are you when they insult you and persecute you and utter every kind of evil against you [falsely] because of me.
12 Rejoice and be glad, for your reward will be great in heaven. Thus they persecuted the prophets who were before you. *(Long pause)*

13 "You are the salt of the earth. But if salt loses its taste, with what can it be seasoned? It is no longer good for anything but to be thrown out and trampled underfoot.
14 You are the light of the world. A city set on a mountain cannot be hidden. *(Long pause)*

15 Nor do they light a lamp and then put it under a bushel basket; it is set on a lampstand, where it gives light to all in the house.
16 Just so, your light must shine before others, that they may see your good deeds and glorify your heavenly Father. *(Long pause)*

17 "Do not think that I have come to abolish the law or the prophets. I have come not to abolish but to fulfill. *(Long pause)*

At the end of 15 minutes, say:

Leader: To continue, please turn to "Prayer" on page 28 in your book.

November

Communal Scripture Meditation as Lectio Divina

Leader: To harmonize with Ordinary Time, we will now meditate on the 3rd Luminous Mystery, the Proclamation of the Gospel, beginning with Lk. 16:19.

(Pause)

Reading

Leader: O Blessed Mother, what does this Scripture say? *(basado en Verbum Domini, Pope Benedict XVI)*

19 "There was a rich man who dressed in purple garments and fine linen and dined sumptuously each day.
20 And lying at his door was a poor man named Lazarus, covered with sores,
21 who would gladly have eaten his fill of the scraps that fell from the rich man's table. Dogs even used to come and lick his sores.

(Pause)

Meditation

Leader: O Blessed Mother, what does this Scripture say to us, personally? *(based on Verbum Domini)*

(Long pause) (a long pause equals approximately 20 seconds)

Reading

Leader: O Blessed Mother, what does this Scripture say?

22 When the poor man died, he was carried away by angels to the bosom of Abraham. The rich man also died and was buried,
23 and from the netherworld, where he was in torment, he raised his eyes and saw Abraham far off and Lazarus at his side.

(Pause)

Meditation

Leader: O Blessed Mother, what does this Scripture say to us, personally?

(Long pause)

Reading and Meditation

The leader will continue reading Scripture verses and pausing, without asking questions, until the next mystery. The faithful may continue to ask themselves the two questions silently after each Scripture reading.

24 And he cried out, 'Father Abraham, have pity on me. Send Lazarus to dip the tip of his finger in water and cool my tongue, for I am suffering torment in these flames.'
25 Abraham replied, 'My child, remember that you received what was good during your lifetime while Lazarus likewise received what was bad; but now he is comforted here, whereas you are tormented. *(Long pause)*

After each reading, silently ask:
O Blessed Mother, what does this Scripture say?
O Blessed Mother, what does this Scripture say to me, personally?

26 Moreover, between us and you a great chasm is established to prevent anyone from crossing who might wish to go from our side to yours or from your side to ours.'
27 He said, 'Then I beg you, father, send him to my father's house,
28 for I have five brothers, so that he may warn them, lest they too come to this place of torment.' *(Long pause)*

29 But Abraham replied, 'They have Moses and the prophets. Let them listen to them.'
30 He said, 'Oh no, father Abraham, but if someone from the dead goes to them, they will repent.'
31 Then Abraham said, 'If they will not listen to Moses and the prophets, neither will they be persuaded if someone should rise from the dead.'" *(Long pause)*

Leader: Keeping in mind the suffering souls in Purgatory, we will now meditate on the 2nd Sorrowful Mystery, the Scourging of Jesus at the Pillar, beginning with Mt. 27:24.

(Pause)

Reading

Leader: O Blessed Mother, what does this Scripture say?

24 So when Pilate saw that he was gaining nothing, but rather that a riot was beginning, he took water and washed his hands before the crowd, saying, "I am innocent of this righteous man's blood; see to it yourselves."

(Pause)

Meditation

Leader: O Blessed Mother, what does this Scripture say to us, personally?

(Long pause)

Reading and Meditation

The leader will continue reading Scripture verses and pausing, without asking questions. The faithful may continue to ask themselves the two questions silently after each Scripture reading.

25 And all the people answered, "His blood be on us and on our children!" 26 Then he released for them Barab'bas, and having scourged Jesus, delivered him to be crucified. *(Long pause)*

Leader: We now continue with passages from Is. 53.

91

53 Who has believed what we have heard? And to whom has the arm of the LORD been revealed?

² For he grew up before him like a young plant, and like a root out of dry ground; he had no form or comeliness that we should look at him, and no beauty that we should desire him. *(Long pause)*

³ He was despised and rejected by men; a man of sorrows, and acquainted with grief; and as one from whom men hide their faces he was despised, and we esteemed him not. *(Long pause)*

⁴ Surely he has borne our griefs and carried our sorrows; yet we esteemed him stricken, smitten by God, and afflicted. ⁵ But he was wounded for our transgressions, he was bruised for our iniquities; upon him was the chastisement that made us whole, and with his stripes we are healed. *(Long pause)*

⁶ All we like sheep have gone astray; we have turned every one to his own way; and the LORD has laid on him the iniquity of us all. *(Long pause)*

⁷ He was oppressed, and he was afflicted, yet he opened not his mouth; like a lamb that is led to the slaughter, and like a sheep that before its shearers is dumb, so he opened not his mouth. *(Long pause)*

⁸ By oppression and judgment he was taken away; and as for his generation, who considered that he was cut off out of the land of the living, stricken for the transgression of my people? ⁹ And they made his grave with the wicked and with a rich man in his death, although he had done no violence, and there was no deceit in his mouth. *(Long pause)*

¹⁰ Yet it was the will of the LORD to bruise him; he has put him to grief; when he makes himself an offering for sin, he shall see his offspring, he shall prolong his days; the will of the LORD shall prosper in his hand; *(Long pause)*

¹¹ he shall see the fruit of the travail of his soul and be satisfied; by his knowledge shall the righteous one, my servant, make many to be accounted righteous; and he shall bear their iniquities. *(Long pause)*

¹² Therefore I will divide him a portion with the great, and he shall divide the spoil with the strong; because he poured out his soul to death, and was numbered with the transgressors; yet he bore the sin of many, and made intercession for the transgressors. *(Long pause)*

Leader: We will now meditate on the 3rd Sorrowful Mystery, the Crowning of Jesus with Thorns, beginning with Mt. 27:27.

(Pause)

[27] Then the soldiers of the governor took Jesus into the praetorium, and they gathered the whole battalion before him. [28] And they stripped him and put a scarlet robe upon him, [29] and plaiting a crown of thorns they put it on his head, and put a reed in his right hand. And kneeling before him they mocked him, saying, "Hail, King of the Jews!" *(Long pause)*

[30] And they spat upon him, and took the reed and struck him on the head. [31] And when they had mocked him, they stripped him of the robe, and put his own clothes on him, and led him away to crucify him. *(Long pause)*

Leader: We now continue with passages from Is. 50.

[5] The Lord GOD has opened my ear, and I was not rebellious, I turned not backward. [6] I gave my back to the smiters, and my cheeks to those who pulled out the beard; I hid not my face from shame and spitting. *(Long pause)*

[7] For the Lord GOD helps me; therefore I have not been confounded; therefore I have set my face like a flint, and I know that I shall not be put to shame; *(Long pause)*

[8] he who vindicates me is near. Who will contend with me? Let us stand up together. Who is my adversary? Let him come near to me. [9] Behold, the Lord GOD helps me; who will declare me guilty? Behold, all of them will wear out like a garment; the moth will eat them up. *(Long pause)*

At the end of 15 minutes, say:

Leader: To continue, please turn to "Prayer" on page 28 in your book.

December

Communal Scripture Meditation as Lectio Divina

Leader: To harmonize with the liturgical season of Advent, we will now meditate on the 1st Joyful Mystery, the Annunciation of the Lord, beginning with Lk. 1:26.

(Pause)

Reading

Leader: O Blessed Mother, what does this Scripture say? *(basado en Verbum Domini, Pope Benedict XVI)*

26 In the sixth month, the angel Gabriel was sent from God to a town of Galilee called Nazareth,
27 to a virgin betrothed to a man named Joseph, of the house of David, and the virgin's name was Mary.

(Pause)

Meditation

Leader: O Blessed Mother, what does this Scripture say to us, personally? *(based on Verbum Domini)*

(Long pause) (a long pause equals approximately 20 seconds)

Reading

Leader: O Blessed Mother, what does this Scripture say?

28 And coming to her, he said, "Hail, favored one [full of grace]! The Lord is with you." *(Brackets are ours)*
29 But she was greatly troubled at what was said and pondered what sort of greeting this might be.

(Pause)

Meditation

Leader: O Blessed Mother, what does this Scripture say to us, personally?

94

(Long pause)

Reading and Meditation

The leader will continue reading Scripture verses and pausing, without asking questions, until the next mystery. The faithful may continue to ask themselves the two questions silently after each Scripture reading.

30 Then the angel said to her, "Do not be afraid, Mary, for you have found favor with God.

31 Behold, you will conceive in your womb and bear a son, and you shall name him Jesus. *(Long pause)*

After each reading, silently ask:
O Blessed Mother, what does this Scripture say?
O Blessed Mother, what does this Scripture say to me, personally?

32 He will be great and will be called Son of the Most High, and the Lord God will give him the throne of David his father,

33 and he will rule over the house of Jacob forever, and of his kingdom there will be no end." *(Long pause)*

34 But Mary said to the angel, "How can this be, since I have no relations with a man?"

35 And the angel said to her in reply, "The holy Spirit will come upon you, and the power of the Most High will overshadow you. Therefore the child to be born will be called holy, the Son of God. *(Long pause)*

36 And behold, Elizabeth, your relative, has also conceived a son in her old age, and this is the sixth month for her who was called barren;

37 for nothing will be impossible for God." *(Long pause)*

38 Mary said, "Behold, I am the handmaid of the Lord. May it be done to me according to your word." Then the angel departed from her. *(Long pause)*

Leader: We will now meditate on the 2nd Joyful Mystery, the Visitation of Mary to Elizabeth, beginning with Lk. 1:39.

(Pause)

Reading

Leader: O Blessed Mother, what does this Scripture say?

39 During those days Mary set out and traveled to the hill country in haste to a town of Judah,
40 where she entered the house of Zechariah and greeted Elizabeth.

(Pause)

Meditation

Leader: O Blessed Mother, what does this Scripture say to us, personally?

(Long pause)

Reading and Meditation

The leader will continue reading Scripture verses and pausing, without asking questions. The faithful may continue to ask themselves the two questions silently after each Scripture reading.

41 When Elizabeth heard Mary's greeting, the infant leaped in her womb, and Elizabeth, filled with the holy Spirit,
42 cried out in a loud voice and said, "Most blessed are you among women, and blessed is the fruit of your womb. *(Long pause)*

43 And how does this happen to me, that the mother of my Lord should come to me?
44 For at the moment the sound of your greeting reached my ears, the infant in my womb leaped for joy. *(Long pause)*

45 Blessed are you who believed that what was spoken to you by the Lord would be fulfilled."
46 And Mary said: "My soul proclaims the greatness of the Lord;
47 my spirit rejoices in God my savior. *(Long pause)*

48 For he has looked upon his handmaid's lowliness; behold, from now on will all ages call me blessed.
49 The Mighty One has done great things for me, and holy is his name.

50 His mercy is from age to age to those who fear him. *(Long pause)*

51 He has shown might with his arm, dispersed the arrogant of mind and heart.
52 He has thrown down the rulers from their thrones but lifted up the lowly.
53 The hungry he has filled with good things; the rich he has sent away empty.
(Long pause)

54 He has helped Israel his servant, remembering his mercy,
55 according to his promise to our fathers, to Abraham and to his descendants forever."
56 Mary remained with her about three months and then returned to her home.
(Long pause)

Leader: We now continue with passages from Lk. 1.

67 Then Zechariah his father, filled with the holy Spirit, prophesied, saying:
68 "Blessed be the Lord, the God of Israel,
for he has visited and brought redemption to his people. *(Long pause)*

69 He has raised up a horn for our salvation
within the house of David his servant,
70 even as he promised through the mouth of his holy prophets from of old:
(Long pause)

71 salvation from our enemies and from the hand of all who hate us,
72 to show mercy to our fathers
and to be mindful of his holy covenant
73 and of the oath he swore to Abraham our father, *(Long pause)*

and to grant us that,
74 rescued from the hand of enemies, without fear we might worship him
75 in holiness and righteousness before him all our days. *(Long pause)*

76 And you, child, will be called prophet of the Most High,
for you will go before the Lord to prepare his ways,
77 to give his people knowledge of salvation
through the forgiveness of their sins, *(Long pause)*

78 because of the tender mercy of our God
by which the daybreak from on high will visit us

79 to shine on those who sit in darkness and death's shadow,
to guide our feet into the path of peace." *(Long pause)*

At the end of 15 minutes, say:

Leader: To continue, please turn to "Prayer" on page 28 in your book.

Appendix I

The Pilgrim Virgin Statue Church to Home Visitation

The Order of Devotion for the Pilgrim Virgin Statue Church to Home Visitation

To Establish the Reign of the Sacred Heart of Jesus in the Home and Bring Us Closer to Him in the Holy Eucharist

1. The Reception of the Pilgrim Virgin Statue in the Church

Leader: Before this devotion begins in the church, please review the first page of Appendix A in "The Communal First Saturdays" book as well as the related information in Appendices F and G of the same book.

The reception of the Pilgrim Virgin statue on the First Saturdays

*The Pilgrim Virgin statue custodian (PVS custodian or other leader) would read the part of the **narrator**. The person reading the part of **Mary** (the person returning the statue that week if possible) and the person reading the part of **Elizabeth** (the person receiving the statue that week if possible) and their family members stand at the foot of the sanctuary. If there are other host(s) whether as individuals or families receiving a statue or other image, they should also stand at the foot of the sanctuary. It is recommended that these additional images be covered and carefully placed on a nearby table or in the first pew.*

The narrator also stands at the foot of the sanctuary.

Narrator: Please turn to page 101 in your books to follow along.

The narrator says the following if there is more than one image of Our Lady present at the reception:

Narrator: (There is more than one image of Our Lady present at the reception this week. The additional image(s) will be covered so that our attention will be focused on one image.)

The following is said whether there are one or more images to be returned and/or received:

Narrator: We ask that anyone who is returning and/or receiving an image of Our Lady come to the foot of the sanctuary.

Narrator: Before we begin, let us try to think of the Pilgrim Virgin statue coming from the sanctuary to the foot of the sanctuary as representing Our Lady's journey from Nazareth to the house of Zechariah on a mission of mercy.

The narrator leads the person reading Mary's part from the foot of the sanctuary to the main Pilgrim Virgin statue in the sanctuary. Both bow to the Blessed Sacrament if present. The person reading the part of Elizabeth should stand near the foot of the sanctuary.

The narrator or an assistant would then present the Pilgrim Virgin statue to the person reading the part of Mary.

The narrator continues:

Narrator: "In those days Mary arose and went with haste into the hill country, to a city of Judah" *(Pause)*

After they both bow to the Blessed Sacrament (if present), the narrator then accompanies the person reading Mary's part to meet the person reading Elizabeth's part at the foot of the sanctuary. In doing so, the person reading Mary's part brings the Pilgrim Virgin statue to the foot of the sanctuary representing Mary's journey to the house of Zechariah.

Narrator: "...and she entered the house of Zechari'ah and greeted Elizabeth. And when Elizabeth heard the greeting of Mary the child leaped in her womb; and Elizabeth was filled with the Holy Spirit and she exclaimed with a loud cry,

Elizabeth: 'Blessed are you among women, and blessed is the fruit of your womb! And why is this granted me, that the mother of my Lord should come to me? For behold, when the voice of your greeting came to my ears, the child in my womb leaped for joy. And blessed is she who believed that there would be a fulfilment of what was spoken to her from the Lord.'"

Narrator: "And Mary said:

Mary: 'My soul magnifies the Lord;

102

and my spirit rejoices in God my Savior,

All: for he has regarded the low estate of his
handmaiden.
For behold, henceforth all generations will call me
blessed;
for he who is mighty has done great things for me,
and holy is his name.
And his mercy is on those who fear him
from generation to generation.
He has shown strength with his arm,
he has scattered the proud in the imagination of their
hearts,
he has put down the mighty from their thrones,
and exalted those of low degree;
he has filled the hungry with good things,
and the rich he has sent empty away.
He has helped his servant Israel,
in remembrance of his mercy,
as he spoke to our fathers,
to Abraham and to his posterity forever.'"

(Pause)

*The narrator now addresses the person who read the part of
Mary:*

Narrator: Please present the Pilgrim Virgin statue to the next
host, _____(*name of host*).

The Pilgrim Virgin statue is presented to the new host.

*As the Pilgrim Virgin statue(s) and/or image(s) is/are presented
to the next host(s), the narrator says:*

Narrator: Receive the Pilgrim Virgin statue. *(Pause)*

Narrator: "And Mary remained with her about three months,
and returned to her home" *(Lk. 1:39-56). (Pause)*

Narrator: As Our Lady brought Jesus into the home of Elizabeth and Zechariah and by the Holy Spirit, Elizabeth acknowledged the real presence of Jesus in Mary, so now Our Lady wishes to bring the Sacred Heart of Jesus into our homes and then bring us back to the real presence of Jesus in the Mass.

Without words, any additional covered Pilgrim Virgin statues or images would be presented to the other new host(s) as well.

Narrator: Please turn your books to page 104 for the hymn, "Immaculate Mary." You may follow behind the procession if you wish.

After bowing in front of the Blessed Sacrament (if present), the narrator, new host(s) and any new host family members begin to process toward the narthex/vestibule.[1][1] The previous host(s) and any family members present proceed next, followed by the congregation.

While processing, all sing "Immaculate Mary" or other approved Marian hymn.

Immaculate Mary

All: Immaculate Mary, your praises we sing;
You reign now in splendor with Jesus our King.
Ave, ave, ave, Maria! Ave, ave, Maria!

In heaven, the blessed your glory proclaim;
On earth we, your children, invoke your sweet name.
Ave, ave, ave, Maria! Ave, ave, Maria!

---

[1] *The new host(s) would then place the statue(s) on a table. The PVS custodian would then 1) place the statue(s) in the protective carrier(s) and 2) before the carrier is closed, point out any helpful related materials, and 3) especially ask the host(s) to look at Appendix A of "The Communal First Saturdays" book, so the host(s) can find information regarding what can take place in the home as well as read and develop an understanding of the meaning of the Pilgrim Virgin statue and the enthronement of the Sacred Heart of Jesus. (If the enthronement of the Sacred Heart of Jesus has already taken place, it is recommended that the enthronement be renewed with each visitation).*

We pray for the Church, our true Mother on earth,
And beg you to watch o'er the land of our birth.
Ave, ave, ave, Maria! Ave, ave, Maria!

After the procession comes to a halt in the designated place (such as the narthex/vestibule), the narrator could announce how one can schedule the Pilgrim Virgin Statue Church to Home Visitation and/or receive First Saturdays information. The following are examples of wording:

Narrator:

- "For those of you who would like to open your homes to the Pilgrim Virgin Statue Church to Home Visitation for a week, you may sign up in the _____(designated place such as the narthex/vestibule)."

- "There is a pamphlet *(hold up "The Pilgrim Virgin Statue Church to Home Visitation" pamphlet)* that explains more about this as well as the enthronement of the Sacred Heart of Jesus that can take place in the home."

- "If you would like First Saturdays information and updates, there is also a 2nd sign up sheet for you to give your name and email."

Other applicable announcements and closing:

- *Announce where the Brown Scapular may be received.*

- *Announce where to return the books.*

- *Announce that the Pilgrim Virgin statue will now be prepared for transportation.*

- *Thank the faithful for coming and ask them to come again to the next Communal First Saturdays.*

The host then proceeds to the place where the image of Our Lady will remain for one week. If a Pilgrim Virgin statue is going to a nursing home, please consult Appendix B of the book mentioned above.

The reception of the Pilgrim Virgin statue on other Saturdays

After Mass, if applicable, after the priest has processed out, the Pilgrim Virgin statue (PVS) custodian would then 1) bring the protective carrier(s) with the statue(s) to a table in the designated place for the reception, 2) set the statue(s) on the table, and 3) place, as recommended, a cover on all statues except one. In the presence of the host receiving the statue the PVS custodian would then begin:

> *PVS custodian:*
>
> > In the Name of the Father and of the Son and of the Holy Spirit. Amen.
> >
> > Let us recall the following words from Scripture: "In those days Mary arose and went with haste into the hill country, to a city of Judah" *(Pause).*
> >
> > Receiving the Pilgrim Virgin statue symbolizes that we receive Our Lady who goes out from the Mass to bring the Sacred Heart of Jesus into our homes. *(Pause)*
> >
> > In the Name of the Father and of the Son and of the Holy Spirit. Amen.

The PVS custodian would then 1) place the statue(s) in the protective carrier(s), and 2) before the carrier is closed, point out any helpful related materials, and 3) especially ask the host(s) to look at Appendix A of "The Communal First Saturdays" book, so the host(s) can find information regarding what can take place in the home as well as read and develop an understanding of the meaning of the Pilgrim Virgin statue and the enthronement of the Sacred Heart of Jesus. (If the enthronement of the Sacred Heart of Jesus has already taken place, it is recommended that the enthronement be renewed with each visitation).

The host then proceeds to the place where the image of Our Lady will remain for one week. If a Pilgrim Virgin statue is going to a nursing home, please consult Appendix B of the book mentioned above.

2. The Return of the Pilgrim Virgin Statue to the Church

Leader: Before you start this devotion in the church, please review "The Communal First Saturdays" book, Appendix A, Section One, 5. The Return of the Pilgrim Virgin Statue to the Church, as well as related information in Appendix F of the same book.

The Pilgrim Virgin statue custodian (PVS custodian) greets the host(s) returning the Pilgrim Virgin statue(s). The host(s) returning the Pilgrim Virgin statue(s) would present the statue(s) to the PVS custodian at the designated area. The PVS custodian would then place one statue on a nearby table. The PVS custodian would then say the following:

PVS custodian:

In the Name of the Father and of the Son and of the Holy Spirit. Amen.

Welcome Blessed Mother and your children (*or child*)! For you, Mary, carried our Savior in your womb. "Blessed are you among women, and blessed is the fruit of your womb." *(Pause)* Let us call to mind that returning the Pilgrim Virgin statue before Mass symbolizes Our Lady bringing the faithful to the Eucharistic Heart of Jesus present in the Mass.

(Pause)

Our Lady visited your home to bring you to the Heart of her Son Jesus and brought you back to the church to be more closely united with His Eucharistic Heart. Our Lady has obtained many other blessings for you. Our Lady has consoled you by her Maternal love for you.

Is there anything we can do for Our Lady in return? *(Pause)* Jesus has asked us to console Him and His Mother for the sins that offend them at every moment. Our Lord and His Mother have asked us to do this by trying to make reparation to her Immaculate Heart for the sins that have pierced her Heart. Our Lord and Our Lady have asked us to try to make reparation to her Immaculate Heart in a special way by making the First Saturdays.

The *Communal First Saturdays* here at (*name of parish or community*) makes this easier to do. You can be sure that in fulfilling the First Saturdays, there will be even greater blessings upon you and your family.

Then the PVS custodian could present to the returning host(s) a printed invitation to the next Communal First Saturdays together with an informational pamphlet on the Communal First Saturdays (pamphlet found at www.CommunalFirstSaturdays.org).

One uncovered Pilgrim Virgin statue would then be temporarily displayed in the designated area. If there is more than one Pilgrim Virgin statue, it is recommended that only one of the statues be uncovered so that the faithful can focus on one image.

Appendix II

The Reception of the Brown Scapular

Guidelines for the Reception of the Brown Scapular

The reception of the Brown Scapular may take place at the end of the Communal First Saturdays. If there is a reception of the Pilgrim Virgin statue, the reception of the Brown Scapular would follow immediately. Please ensure the announcement regarding the reception of the Brown Scapular is read after the recitation of the Rosary. Please see page 23.

Only a person authorized by the Carmelite Order may enroll the faithful in the Confraternity of Our Lady of Mt. Carmel. For enrollment in the Confraternity of Our Lady of Mt. Carmel, one can contact the Carmelite Order. However, there are other forms of affiliation with the Carmelite Order. One may simply receive and/or wear a blessed Brown Scapular with the intention of living according to the meaning of the Scapular. One may "receive" a blessed Brown Scapular from anyone, but it is still important for the recipient to have some preparation. It is strongly recommended that the pamphlet, "The Brown Scapular," be made available to the faithful at the Communal First Saturdays to assist with preparation. This pamphlet is available at www.Communal FirstSaturdays.org. We recommend that when children reach the age of reason, or seven years old, parents may prepare them for receiving the Scapular with the aid of the same pamphlet. This is a wonderful opportunity for the family to reflect consciously on the meaning of their Baptism.

With the permission of the pastor, lay leaders of the Communal First Saturdays may bestow blessed Brown Scapulars on the faithful. The prayers for the reception are found below. The leader may say the following prayers once for one or more recipients and then place the Brown Scapular on each of the recipient(s).

Reception of the Scapular

Leader: Dear children (*or child*) of our Blessed Mother, if any of you (*if you*) have not read this Brown Scapular pamphlet [*hold up the pamphlet*], we recommend that you read it as soon as possible, so you can understand more of what the Brown Scapular means, and so you can wear the Scapular with the proper dispositions.

We recommend that when a child reaches the age of reason or seven years old, he or she may receive the Scapular. If a child who has reached the age of reason or is seven years old wishes to receive the Scapular, ask the parent(s) for his/her/their permission. If permission is given, ask the parent(s) if he/she/they will read the pamphlet and instruct the child.

All:

    1. In the Name of the Father...

    2. Hail Mary...

Leader:

    3. Receive this blessed Scapular, a sign of your special relationship with Mary the Mother of Jesus, whom you pledge to imitate. May it be a reminder of your baptismal vows and of your dignity as a Christian, in serving others and imitating Mary. Wear it as a sign of her protection, voluntarily doing the will of God and devoting yourself to building a world true to His plan of community, justice and peace. Finally, wear this Scapular as a sign of your consecration to the Immaculate Heart of Mary.

    4. *As you place the Brown Scapular on the person, say the following:*

    Receive this blessed Scapular.

    5. In the Name of the Father...

Appendix III

Hymns

Hymns

These hymns are included here for your convenience. The leader is free to choose other approved hymns.

Hail, Holy Queen Enthroned Above

Hail, holy Queen enthroned above, O Maria.
Hail, Queen of mercy and of love, O Maria.
Triumph, all ye cherubim, Sing with us, ye seraphim,
Heaven and earth resound the hymn:
Salve, salve, salve Regina!

The cause of joy to men below, O Maria.
The spring through which all graces flow, O Maria.
Angels, all your praises bring, Earth and heaven, with us sing,
All creation echoing:
Salve, salve, salve Regina!

Immaculate Mary

Immaculate Mary, your praises we sing;
You reign now in splendor with Jesus our King.
Ave, ave, ave, Maria! Ave, ave, Maria!

In heaven, the blessed your glory proclaim;
On earth we, your children, invoke your sweet name.
Ave, ave, ave, Maria! Ave, ave, Maria!

We pray for the Church, our true Mother on earth,
And beg you to watch o'er the land of our birth.
Ave, ave, ave, Maria! Ave, ave, Maria!

O Sanctissima

O sanctissima, o piissima,
dulcis Virgo Maria!
Mater amata, intemerata,
ora, ora pro nobis.

Tu solatium et refugium,
Virgo Mater Maria.
Quidquid optamus, per te speramus;
ora, ora pro nobis.

Ecce debiles, perquam flebiles;
salva nos, o Maria!
Tolle languores, sana dolores;
ora, ora pro nobis.

Virgo, respice, Mater, aspice;
audi nos, o Maria!
Tu medicinam portas divinam;
ora, ora pro nobis.

Contact Information

For more information or questions, please contact:
Communal First Saturdays Apostolate
www.CommunalFirstSaturdays.org
Email:
info@communalfirstsaturdays.org

Made in the USA
Coppell, TX
06 October 2021

63596555R00069